50
Communication Strategies

Joseph A. DeVito

iUniverse, Inc.
Bloomington

50 Communication Strategies

iUniverse books may be ordered through booksellers or by contacting:

iUniverse
1663 Liberty Drive
Bloomington, IN 47403
www.iuniverse.com
1-800-Authors (1-800-288-4677)

ISBN: 978-1-4759-5650-4 (sc)
ISBN: 978-1-4759-5652-8 (e)
ISBN: 978-1-4759-5651-1 (dj)

Library of Congress Control Number: 2012919645

Printed in the United States of America

iUniverse rev. date: 10/22/2012

Table of Contents

Welcome to

50 Communication Strategies

50 Communication Strategies has a very modest aim and that is to identify important communication strategies to make your own communications (written or oral, face-to-face or online) more effective, more persuasive, more powerful, more memorable.

This book is purposely brief, despite its 50 chapters. In contrast to the literature on which this material is based, this book is very, very brief. The theoretical and research literature from which this material is derived is voluminous. The college textbooks I've written on human communication, interpersonal communication, nonverbal communication, interviewing, and public speaking, which cover only a small part of the communication literature, often run to five hundred pages. The book you're holding is a distillation of this material into a form that focuses on the strategies you can use to communicate more effectively.

Some of the 50 chapters are very short; others are a bit longer. Instead of padding the short ones or cutting important material from the long ones, they are here in different lengths simply because each chapter deals with a different topic; some topics require more explanation and offer more strategies than others.

Each chapter is separate and distinct (hence their appearance in alphabetical order) and is designed to help you achieve one communication goal. Hence, the chapters may be read in any order; select and choose according to your own communication needs.

Each chapter has a simple, straightforward structure and contains the concept (a communication goal, actually), a brief explanation, bulleted strategies for achieving this goal, and a brief reminder (called, *Try It*) to use this material in your own communications. In about half of the chapters an *& Box* is included. These provide added insights into the chapter's concept and may be read or skipped as you wish. In most cases, I think, you'll find these boxes both interesting and useful.

The strategies identified and discussed throughout the book are repeated in brief in the *In a Nutshell* section at the end of the book. Its purpose is to provide a quick review and memory joggers.

At the end of the book is a list of references which is designed to serve two main purposes: First and foremost, it allows me the opportunity to acknowledge the sources I used and to whom the credit should go. Nothing here is original with me (well, perhaps a little). Here I function as a teacher and reporter, rather than as a researcher or theorist. These are the topics that I taught at Lehman, Queens, and Hunter Colleges for some thirty years and about which I've written college textbooks for an even longer time. In addition, these references will provide a useful guide for anyone who cares to pursue one or more of the topics in greater depth.

In order to apply these communication strategies most effectively, some knowledge of how communication works is necessary. Here are ten things you need to know about communication. Understanding these ten simple "principles" will help you apply the strategies more appropriately and more effectively.

Communication Is Inherently Relational

Communication is inevitably and essentially relational in nature. Communication creates a relationship between or among the people interacting. Communication takes place in a relationship, it affects the relationship, it defines the relationship. The way you communicate is determined in great part by the kind of relationship that exists between you and the other person. You interact differently with your supermarket cashier and your best friend; you interact with a sibling in ways very different from the ways you interact with a neighbor, a work colleague, or a casual acquaintance.

But notice also that the way you communicate will influence the kind of relationship you have. If you interact in friendly ways, you're likely to develop a friendship. If you regularly exchange hateful and hurtful messages, you're likely to develop an antagonistic relationship. If you each regularly express respect and support for each other, a respectful and supportive relationship is likely to develop. This is surely one of the most obvious observations you can make about interpersonal communication. And yet so many seem not to appreciate this very clear relationship between what you say and the relationship that develops (or deteriorates).

Communication Involves Verbal and Nonverbal Messages

Communication takes place on both verbal and nonverbal levels, usually at the same time. Communication involves the exchange of both verbal and nonverbal messages. The words you use as well as your nonverbal behaviors—your eye contact, facial expressions, and your body posture, for example—send messages. Likewise, you receive messages through your sense of hearing as well as through your other senses, especially visual and touch. Even silence sends messages. One of the great myths in communication is that nonverbal communication accounts for more than 90 percent of the meaning of any message. Actually, it depends. In some situations, the nonverbal signals will carry more of your meaning than the words you use. In other situations, the verbal signals will communicate more information. Most often, of course, they work together, and, rather than focusing on which channel communicates the greater percentage of meaning, it's more important to focus on the ways in which verbal and nonverbal messages occur together.

Communication Involves Choices

Throughout your communication experiences you're presented with choice points—moments when you have to make a choice as to who you communicate with, what you say, what you don't say, how you phrase what you want to say, and so on. You can look at the process of choice in terms of John Dewey's steps in reflective thinking, a model used by contemporary theorists for explaining small group problem solving and conflict resolution. It can also be used to explain the notion of choice in five steps.

- **Step 1. The problem.** View a communication interaction as a problem to be resolved, as a situation to be addressed. Here you'd try to understand the nature of the communication situation. What elements are involved? Let's say that your "problem" is that you said something you shouldn't have and it's created a rift between you and your friend, romantic partner, or family member. You need to resolve this problem.
- **Step 2. The criteria.** Here you ask yourself what your specific communication goal is. What do you want your message to accomplish? For example, you might want to admit your mistake, apologize, and be forgiven.

- **Step 3. The possible solutions**. Here you ask yourself what are some of your communication choices. What are some of the messages you might communicate to accomplish your goal.
- **Step 4. The analysis.** Here you identify the advantages and disadvantages of each communication choice.
- **Step 5. The selection and execution.** Here you communicate what you hope will resolve the problem and get you forgiveness.

Of course, you don't do this so analytically, nor do you do this at all times—there's usually no reason to over think most of our communications. But, when the stakes are high and—to stick with our example—a life-long friendship may be destroyed, it's helpful to recognize that you have choices and that you can analyze most communication situations systematically.

Communication Is Purposeful

Communication always serves a purpose. It is, by nature, a purposeful act. You may not always be conscious of your reasons for communicating but with a little reflection you'll no doubt find purpose behind your messages. One of the major purposes is to relate to other people and to form meaningful relationships whether it's face to face or online. Such relationships help to alleviate loneliness and depression, enable you to share and heighten your pleasures, and generally make you feel more positive about yourself. Another major purpose is to persuade, to influence the attitudes and behaviors of others. Sometimes the persuasion concerns minor issues--to try a new recipe or to see a movie—and sometimes the persuasion is highly significant—to marry you, to get you a job or promotion, for example. Still another important function is to help another person. Therapists serve this function professionally, but everyone interacts to help in everyday life: Online and offline, you console a friend who has broken off a love affair, counsel a student about courses to take, or offer advice to a colleague at work. Sometimes communication serves a simple playful function—tweeting your weekend activities or discussing sports or dates or posting a clever joke on some social media site. Regardless of what the specific purpose is, it's important to recognize that there is a purpose or purposes to all communication.

Communication Is a Package of Signals

Communication behaviors, whether they involve verbal messages, gestures, or some combination thereof, usually occur in "packages". Usually, verbal and nonverbal behaviors reinforce or support each other. All parts of a message system normally work together to communicate a particular meaning. You don't express fear with words while the rest of your body is relaxed. You don't express anger through your posture while your face smiles. Your entire body works together—verbally and nonverbally—to express your thoughts and feelings.

You probably pay little attention to its "packaged" nature unless there's an incongruity—when the chilly handshake belies the verbal greeting, when the nervous posture belies the focused stare, when the constant preening belies the expressions of being comfortable and at ease—you take notice. Invariably you begin to question the credibility, the sincerity, and the honesty of the individual.

Communication Involves Content *and* Relationship Messages

Communication can be viewed in terms of content and relationship messages. Content messages focus on the real world, to something external to both speaker and listener. Relationship messages, on the other hand, focus on the relationship/connection between the individuals. For example, a supervisor may say to a trainee, "See me after the meeting." This simple message has a content message that tells the trainee to see the supervisor after the meeting. It also contains a relationship message that says something about the connection between the supervisor and the trainee. Even the use of the simple command shows there is a status difference that allows the supervisor to command the trainee. You can appreciate this most clearly if you visualize this command being made by the trainee to the supervisor. It appears awkward and out of place, because it violates the normal relationship between supervisor and trainee.

Deborah Tannen, in her book *You're Wearing That?*, gives lots of examples of content and relationship communication and the problems that can result from different interpretations. For example, the mother who says, "Are you going to quarter those tomatoes?" may think she is communicating solely a content message. To the daughter, however, the message is largely relational and is in fact a criticism of the way she intends to cut the tomatoes. Questions, especially, may appear to be objective and focused on content but often are perceived as attacks, as in the title of Tannen's book.

Communication Is Ambiguous

All messages are ambiguous to some degree; messages can be interpreted as having more than one meaning. Sometimes ambiguity results when we use words that can be interpreted differently. Informal time terms offer good examples; different people may interpret terms such as *soon, right away, in a minute, early,* and *late* very differently. The terms themselves are ambiguous.

But some degree of ambiguity exists in all communication. When you express an idea, you never communicate your meaning exactly and totally; rather, you communicate your meaning with some reasonable accuracy—enough to give the other person a reasonably clear idea of what you mean. Sometimes, of course, you're less accurate than you anticipated and your listener "gets the wrong idea" or "gets offended" when you only meant to be humorous, or "misunderstands your emotional meaning." Because of this inevitable uncertainty, you may qualify what you're saying, give an example, or ask, "Do you know what I mean?" These clarifying tactics help the other person understand your meaning and reduce uncertainty (to some degree).

Communication Is Punctuated

Communication interactions are continuous; there is no clear-cut beginning or ending. As a participant in or an observer of the communication act, you engage in punctuation: You divide up this continuous, circular process into causes and effects, or stimuli and responses. That is, you segment this continuous stream of communication into smaller pieces. You label some of these pieces causes, or stimuli, and others effects, or responses.

Consider an example. A married couple is in a restaurant. The husband is flirting with another woman, and the wife is talking to her sister on her cell phone. Both are scowling at each other and are obviously in a deep nonverbal argument. Recalling the situation later, the husband might observe that the wife talked on the phone, so he innocently flirted with the other woman. The only reason for his behavior (he says) was his anger over her talking on the phone when they were supposed to be having dinner together. Notice that he sees his behavior as a response to her behavior. In recalling the same incident, the wife might say that she phoned her sister when he started flirting. The more he flirted, the longer she talked. She had no intention of calling anyone until he started flirting. To her, his behavior was the stimulus and hers was the response; he caused her behavior. Thus, the husband sees the sequence as going from phoning to flirting, and the wife sees it as going from flirting to phoning. This example, interestingly enough, is supported by research showing that, among married couples, the individuals regularly see their partner's behavior as the cause of conflict. This tendency to divide up the various communication transactions in sequences of stimuli and responses is referred to as **punctuation of communication.** People punctuate the continuous sequences of events into stimuli and responses for ease of understanding and remembering.

Communication Is Polite (Usually)

Politeness figures into a wide variety of communication situations (as you'll see in the coming chapters) and so a few words about politeness-in-general seems in order. We can view politeness in terms of negative and positive types. Both of these types of politeness are responsive to two needs that we each have:

- **positive face**—the desire to be viewed positively by others, to be thought of favorably, to be liked, to be appreciated
- **negative face**—the desire to be autonomous, to have the right to do as we wish, to not be burdened with tasks that must be accomplished

Politeness in communication, then, refers to behavior that allows others to maintain both positive and negative face and impoliteness refers to behaviors that attack either positive face (for example, you criticize someone) or negative face (for example, you make demands on someone). To help another person maintain *positive face,* you speak respectfully to and about the person, you give the person your full attention, and you say "excuse me" when appropriate. In short, you treat the person as you would want to be treated. In this way, you allow the person to maintain positive face through what is called *positive politeness.* You *attack* the person's positive face when you speak disrespectfully about the person, ignore the person or the person's comments, and fail to use the appropriate expressions of politeness such as *thank you* and *please.*

To help another person maintain *negative face,* you respect the person's right to be autonomous and so you request rather than demand that he or she do something; you say, "Would you mind opening a window" rather than "Open that window, damn it!" You might also give the person an "out" when making a request, allowing the person to reject your request if that is what the person wants. And so you say, "If this is a bad time, please tell me, but I'm really strapped and could use a loan of $100" rather than "Loan me a $100" or "You have to lend me $100." If you want a recommendation, you might say, "Would it be possible for you to write me a recommendation for a job?" rather than "You have to write me a recommendation for a job." In this way, you enable the person to maintain negative face through what is called *negative politeness.*

While politeness is responded to positively, over-politeness is not. Overpoliteness is likely to be seen as phony and is likely to be resented. Overpoliteness will be especially resented if it's seen as a persuasive strategy.

Communication is Inevitable, Irreversible, and Unrepeatable

Three characteristics often considered together are communication's *inevitability, irreversibility,* and *unrepeatability.*

- Communication is inevitable Often communication is intentional, purposeful, and consciously motivated. Sometimes, however, you are communicating even though you may not think you are or may not even want to. Take, for example, the student sitting in the back of the room with an "expressionless" face, perhaps staring out the window. The student may think that she or he is not communicating with the teacher or with the other students. On closer inspection, however, you can see that the student *is* communicating something—perhaps lack of interest or simply anxiety about a private problem. In any event, the student is communicating whether she or he wishes to or not—demonstrating the principle of inevitability. Similarly, the color and type of your cell phone, the wallpaper in your room, and the type and power of your computer or cell phone communicate messages about you. You cannot *not* communicate.

- Communication is irreversible Notice that only some processes can be reversed. For example, you can turn water into ice and then reverse the process by turning the ice back into water. Other processes, however, are irreversible. You can, for example, turn grapes into wine, but you cannot reverse the process and turn wine into grapes. Communication is an irreversible process. Although you may try to qualify, deny, or somehow reduce the effects of your message, you cannot withdraw the message you have communicated. Similarly, once you press the send key, your e-mail is in cyberspace and impossible to reverse.
- Communication is unrepeatable The reason why communication is unrepeatable is simple: Everyone and everything are constantly changing. As a result, you never can recapture the exact same situation, frame of mind, or relationship dynamics that defined a previous interpersonal act. For example, you never can repeat meeting someone for the first time, comforting a grieving friend, or resolving a specific conflict. You can, of course, try again; you can say, "I'm sorry I came off so pushy, can we try again?" Notice, however, that even when you say this, you have not erased the initial (and perhaps negative) impression. Instead, you try to counteract this impression by going through the motions again. In doing so, you hope to create a more positive impact that will lessen the original negative effect.

These ten principles of communication will serve you well as you master the fifty strategies to which we now turn. Here's to more effective communication.

Strategies for

Advice Giving and Receiving

Advice is the process of giving another person a suggestion for thinking or behaving, usually to change (but often to strengthen) his or her attitudes, beliefs, or behaviors. The popularity of the "Dear Abby" type of columns in print and in online newspapers and magazines and the many websites that offer advice on just about everything attests to our concern with asking for and getting advice.

In many ways, you can look at advice giving as a suggestion to solve a problem. So, for example, you might advise friends to change their ways of looking at broken love affairs or their financial situations or their career paths. Or you might advise someone to do something, to behave in a certain way, for example, to start dating again or to invest in technology stocks or to go back to school and take advanced courses.

Meta-Advice

Notice that you can give advice in at least two ways. One way is to give specific advice, and another is to give meta-advice, or advice about advice. Thus, you can give advice to a person that addresses the problem or issue directly—buy that condo, take this course, or vacation in Hawaii. But you can also give advice about advice. For example, you might suggest that the individual explore additional options and choices. So, when confronted with a request for advice, this meta-advice would focus on helping the person explore the available options. If a friend asks what he or she should do about never having a date, you might give meta-advice and help your friend explore the available options and the advantages and disadvantages of each. Another type of meta-advice is to suggest the individual seek expert advice. If confronted with a request for advice concerning some technical issue in which you have no competence, the best advice is often meta-advice, in this case, to seek advice from someone who is an expert in the field. When a friend asks what to do about a persistent cough, the best advice seems to be the meta-advice to "talk to your doctor." Still another form of meta-advice is to suggest that the decision be delayed (assuming that it doesn't have to be made immediately). If your advice-seeking friend has two weeks to decide on whether to take a job with XYZ Company, meta-advice would suggest that the decision be delayed while the company is researched more thoroughly.

Giving Advice Here are a few useful strategies for giving specific advice.

- **Listen.** This is the first rule for advice giving. Listen to the person's thoughts and feelings. Listen to what the person wants—the person may actually want a supportive and concerned listener and not advice. Or the person may simply want to vent in the presence of a friend. For more on listening see the *Listening* and *Listening Actively* chapters.

- Empathize. Try to feel what the other person is feeling. Perhaps you might recall similar situations you were in or similar emotions you experienced. Think about the importance of the issue to the person, and, in general, try to put yourself into the position, the circumstance, or the context of the person asking your advice. For more on this see the *Empathy* chapter.

- **Be tentative.** If you give advice, give it with the qualifications it requires. The advice-seeker has a right to know how sure (or unsure) you are of the advice or what evidence (or lack of evidence) you have that the advice will work.

- **Ensure understanding.** Often people seeking advice are emotionally upset and may not remember everything in the conversation. So seek feedback after giving advice, for example, "Does that make sense?" "Is my suggestion workable?"

- **Keep the interaction confidential.** Often advice-seeking is directed at very personal matters, so it's best to keep such conversations confidential, even if you're not asked to do so.

- **Avoid *should* statements.** People seeking advice still have to make their own decisions rather than being told what they should or should not do. So it's better to say, for example, "You *might* do X" or "You *could* do Y" rather than "You *should* do Z." Don't demand—or even imply—that the person has to follow your advice. This attacks the person's negative face, the person's need for autonomy.

Responding to Advice Responding appropriately to advice is an often difficult process. Here are just a few strategies for receiving advice more effectively.

- **Accept the advice.** If you asked for the advice, then accept what the person says. You don't have to follow the advice; you just have to listen to it and process it.

- **Avoid negative responses.** And even if you didn't ask for advice (and don't like it), resist the temptation to retaliate or criticize the advice giver. Instead of responding with "Well, your hair doesn't look that great either," consider if the advice has any merit.

- **Interact with the advice.** Talk about it with the advice-giver. A simple process of asking and answering questions is likely to produce added insight into the problem.

- **Express appreciation.** Express your appreciation for the advice. It's often difficult to give advice, so it's only fair that the advice-giver receive some words of appreciation.

Try It

The next time you find yourself in the position of advice-giver, keep these strategies consciously in mind as you decide whether or not you'll offer advice and if you do offer it, how you'll do it. Do the same the next time you receive advice. You'll likely find that when you follow the strategies for giving and responding to advice that the entire experience will be more profitable and more enjoyable.

Strategies for

Anger Management

Anger is one of the most basic emotions; it's also an emotion that can create considerable problems if not managed properly. Anger varies from mild annoyance to intense rage with increases in pulse rate and blood pressure usually accompanying these feelings.

Anger is not always necessarily bad. In fact, anger may help you protect yourself, energizing you to fight or flee. Often, however, anger does prove destructive—as when, for example, you allow it to obscure reality or to become an obsession.

Anger doesn't just happen; you make it happen by your interpretation of events. Yet life events can contribute mightily. There are the road repairs that force you to detour so you wind up late for an important appointment. There are the moths that attack your favorite sweater. There's the water leak that ruins your carpet. People, too, can contribute to your anger: the driver who tailgates, the clerk who overcharges you, the supervisor who ignores your hard work for the company. But it is you who interpret these events and people in ways that stimulate you to generate anger.

Writing more than a hundred years ago, Charles Darwin observed in his *The Expression of the Emotions in Man and Animals* that "The free expression by outside signs of an emotion intensifies it . . . the repression, as far as this is possible, of all outside signs softens our emotions. He who gives way to violent gestures will increase his rage." Popular psychology ignored Darwin's implied admonition in the 1960s and '70s, when the suggested prescription for dealing with anger was to "let it all hang out" and "tell it like it is." Express your anger, many people advised, or risk its being bottled up and eventually exploding. This idea is called the ventilation hypothesis—the notion that expressing emotions allows you to vent[ilate] your negative feelings and that this will have a beneficial effect on your physical health, your mental well-being, and even your social and personal relationships.

Later thinking has returned to Darwin, however, and suggests that venting anger may not always be the best strategy. Expressing anger doesn't get rid of it but makes it grow: Angry expression increases anger, which promotes more angry expression, which increases anger, and on and on. Some support for this idea that expressing emotions makes them stronger comes from a study that compared (a) participants who felt emotions such as happiness and anger with (b) participants who both felt and expressed these emotions. The results of the study indicated that people who felt and expressed the emotions became emotionally aroused faster than did those who only felt the emotion. And of course this spiral of anger can make conflicts all the more serious and all the more difficult to manage.

Perhaps the most popular recommendation for dealing with anger is to count to 10. The purpose is to give you a cooling-off period, and the advice is not bad. A somewhat more difficult but probably more effective strategy, however, would be to use that cooling-off period not merely for counting but for mindfully analyzing and ultimately managing your anger. See the & Box, SCREAM Before You Scream, for more specific suggestions.

&

SCREAM Before You Scream.

The **anger management** procedure offered here is similar to those available in popular books on anger management but is couched in a communication framework. It's called SCREAM, an acronym for the major components of the communication process that you need to consider: **S**elf, **C**ontext, **R**eceiver, **E**ffect, **A**ftermath, and **M**essages.

Self. How important is this matter to you? Is it worth the high blood pressure and the general aggravation? Are you interpreting the "insult" as the other person intended or could you be misperceiving the situation or the intent? Are you confusing factual with inferential knowledge? Are you sure that what you think happened really happened?

- Context. Is this the appropriate time and place to express your anger? Do you have to express your anger right now? Do you have to express it right here? Might a better time and place be arranged?
- Receiver. Is this person the one to whom you wish to express your anger? For example, do you want to express your anger to your life partner if you're really angry with your supervisor for not recommending your promotion?
- Effect *(immediate)*. What effect do you want to achieve? Do you want to express your anger to help you get the promotion? To hurt the other person? To release pent-up emotions? To stand up for your rights? Each purpose would obviously require a different communication strategy. Consider, too, the likely effect of your anger

display. For example, will the other person also become angry? And if so, is it possible that the entire situation will snowball and get out of hand?

- Aftermath (long-range). What are the likely long-term repercussions of this expression of anger? What will be the effects on your relationship? Your continued employment?
- Messages. Suppose that after this rather thorough analysis, you do decide to express your anger. What messages would be appropriate? How can you best communicate your feelings to achieve your desired results? This question brings us to the subject of anger communication.

Anger communication is not angry communication. In fact, it might be argued that the communication of anger ought to be especially calm and dispassionate. With this in mind, here are a few strategies for communicating your anger in a non-angry way.

- **Get ready to communicate calmly and logically.** Relax. Try to breathe deeply, think pleasant thoughts (perhaps tell yourself to "take it easy," "think rationally," and "calm down"). Try to get rid of any unrealistic ideas you may have that might contribute to your anger. For example, ask yourself if this person's revealing something about your past to a third party is really all that serious or was really intended to hurt you.

- **Examine your communication choices.** In most situations you'll have a range of choices. There are lots of different ways to express yourself, so don't jump to the first possibility that comes to mind. Assess your options for the form of the communication—should you communicate face-to-face? By e-mail? By telephone? Similarly, assess your options for the timing of your communication, for the specific words and gestures you might use, for the physical setting, and so on.

- **Consider the advantages of delaying the expression of anger.** For example, consider writing the e-mail but sending it to yourself, at least until the next morning. Then the options of revising it or not sending it at all will still be open to you.

- **Remember that different cultures have different rules.** These rules establish norms for what is and what is not appropriate to express. Assess the culture you're in as well as the cultures of the other people involved, especially these cultures' rules for expressing anger.

- **Apply the relevant skills of communication.** For example, be specific, be willing to take responsibility for what you say, avoid extreme terms such as *never* and *always*, and in general communicate with all the competence you can muster.

- Recall the irreversibility of communication. Once you say something, you'll not be able to erase or delete it from the mind of the other person. And if you're communicating online, the permanence of your message is even more significant. So assess the possible consequences before you say what's on your mind.

Try It

These strategies are not going to solve the problems of road rage, gang warfare, or domestic violence. Yet they may help—a bit—in reducing some of the negative consequences of anger and perhaps even some of the anger itself. The next time you feel anger, SCREAM before you scream.

Strategies for

Apologizing

Despite your best efforts, there are times when you'll say or do the wrong thing and an apology may be necessary. An apology is an expression of regret or sorrow for having done what you did or for what happened; it's an expression of your being sorry. And so, the most basic of all apologies is simply: *I'm sorry.*

In popular usage, the apology includes some admission of wrongdoing on the part of the person making the apology. Sometimes the wrongdoing is acknowledged explicitly (*I'm sorry I lied*) and sometimes only by implication (*I'm sorry you're so upset*). In many cases the apology also includes a request for forgiveness (*Please excuse my lateness*) and some assurance that this won't happen again (*I'm sorry for being late; it won't happen again*).

An effective apology must be crafted for the specific situation. An effective apology to a longtime lover, to a parent, or to a new supervisor are likely to be very different because the individuals are different and your relationships are different. And so the first rule of an effective apology is to take into consideration the uniqueness of the situation—the people, the context, the cultural rules, the relationship, the specific wrongdoing—for which you might want to apologize. Each situation will call for a somewhat different message of apology. Nevertheless, we can offer some general recommendations.

The Pseudo-Apology

When you apologize, apologize. Here are a few words and phrases you'll want to avoid in making your apology.

- **If**, as in *I'm sorry if I offended you.* This dilutes the apology.
- **I know you think**, as in *I know you think I was inconsiderate; in truth, I was ....* This is just an invitation to an argument.
- **But,** as in a preface to an excuse such as *I'm sorry the figures are late, but I had so much other work to do.* An excuse often takes back the apology and says, in effect, I'm really not sorry because there was good reason for what I did, but I'm saying "I'm sorry" to cover all my bases and to make this uncomfortable situation go away.
- **Whatever,** as in *Whatever I did, it's over.* This denies the importance of the incident and the other person's concern over it.

- **Admit wrongdoing** (if indeed wrongdoing occurred). Accept responsibility. Own your own actions; don't try to pass them off as the work of someone else. Instead of *Smith drives so slow, it's a wonder I'm only 30 minutes late*, say *I should have taken traffic into consideration.*

- **Be apologetic.** Say (and mean) the words *I'm sorry.* Don't justify your behavior by mentioning that everyone does it, for example, *Everyone leaves work early on Friday.* Don't justify your behavior by saying that the other person has done something equally wrong: *So I play poker; you play the lottery.*

- **Be specific.** State, in specific rather than general terms, what you've done. Instead of *I'm sorry for what I did*, say *I'm sorry for flirting at the party.*

- **Empathize.** Express understanding of how the other person feels and acknowledge the legitimacy of these feelings, for example, *You have every right to be angry; I should have called.* Express your regret that this has created a problem for the other person: *I'm sorry I made you miss your appointment.* Don't minimize the problem that this may have caused. Avoid such comments as *So the figures arrived a little late. What's the big deal?* For more on this see the *Empathy* chapter.

- **Give assurance that this will not happen again.** Say, quite simply, *It won't happen again* or, better and more specifically, *I won't be late again.* And, whenever possible, offer to correct the problem: *I'm sorry I didn't clean up the mess I made; I'll do it now.*

- **Choose the appropriate channel.** Don't take the easy way out and apologize through e-mail (unless the wrongdoing was committed in e-mail or if e-mail is your only or main form of communication). Generally, it's more effective to use a more personal mode of communication—face-to-face or phone, for example. It's harder but it's more effective.

Try It

The next time you do something for which you are truly sorry, instead of saying nothing and avoiding the issue, craft an apology following some or all of the strategies offered here. Once crafted, you can decide whether or not to voice it.

Strategies for managing

Apprehension

Many communication situations make people anxious, fearful, apprehensive. Perhaps the public speaking situation is the most anxiety provoking of all but meeting people for the first time, interviewing for a job, or leading a group meeting can also create anxiety. Fortunately, this fear is also something that can be managed and made to work for you rather than against you.

Communication apprehension exists on a continuum. Some people are so apprehensive that they're unable to function effectively in any communication situation and will avoid communication as much as possible. Other people are not apprehensive at all or only mildly so; they're the ones who actively seek out communication opportunities. Most of us are between these extremes.

Contrary to popular belief, apprehension is not necessarily harmful. In fact, apprehension can work for you. Fear can energize you. It may motivate you to work a little harder—to produce a speech or rehearse potential interview questions that will improve your performance. Further, the other person or the audience probably cannot see the apprehension that you may be experiencing. Even though you may think that they can hear your heart beat faster, they can't. They can't see your knees tremble. They can't sense your dry throat—at least not most of the time.

Here are several ways you can deal with and manage your own apprehension.

- **Reverse the factors that cause apprehension** If you can reverse or at least lessen the factors that cause apprehension, you'll be able to reduce your apprehension significantly. The following suggestions are based on research identifying the major factors contributing to your fear in public speaking but they can easily be applied to any anxiety-provoking interaction.
    - **Reduce the newness of the communication by gaining experience.** New and different situations such as public speaking or employment interviewing are likely to make anyone anxious, so try to reduce their newness and differentness. One way to do this is to get as much experience as you can. With experience your initial fears and anxieties will give way to feelings of control and comfort. Experience will show you that the feelings of accomplishment you gain from successful communication experiences are rewarding and will outweigh any initial anxiety.
    - **Reduce your self-focus by visualizing the communication as conversation.** When you're the center of attention, as you are in public speaking or in a job interview, you feel especially conspicuous, and this often increases anxiety. It may help, therefore, to think of these situations as another type of conversation.
    - **Reduce your perceived differentness between yourself and the other person(s).** When you feel similar to (rather than different from) the people to whom you're talking, your anxiety should lessen. Therefore, try to think of the similarities between yourself and others.
    - **Reduce your fear of failure by thoroughly preparing and practicing.** Much of the fear

you experience is a fear of failure. Adequate and even extra preparation will lessen the possibility of failure and the accompanying apprehension.

- **Reduce your anxiety by moving about and breathing deeply.** Physical activity—including movements of the whole body as well as small movements of the hands, face, and head—lessens apprehension. In public speaking, moving about is usually a viable option whereas in interviewing it isn't. Nevertheless, when possible, try to move about at least a bit. Also, try breathing deeply a few times before the meeting or interview or speech. You'll feel your body relax, and this will help you overcome your initial fear.
- **Avoid chemicals as tension relievers.** Unless prescribed by a physician, avoid any chemical means for reducing apprehension. Tranquilizers, marijuana, or artificial stimulants are likely to create problems rather than reduce them. And, of course, alcohol does nothing to reduce apprehension. These chemicals can impair your ability to remember what you want to say and to accurately read the feedback you get from others.

- **Restructure your thinking**. The suggestion to restructure your thinking might at first seem a strange idea. Yet cognitive restructuring or cognitive reappraisal—as the technique is technically known—is a proven technique for reducing a great number of fears and stresses. The general idea behind this technique is that the way you think about a situation influences the way you react to the situation. If you can change the way you think about a situation (reframe it, restructure it, reappraise it) you'll be able to change your reactions to the situation. So, if you think that public speaking will produce stress (fear, apprehension, anxiety), then reappraising it as less threatening will reduce the stress, fear, apprehension, and anxiety.

Much communication apprehension is based on unrealistic thinking, on thinking that is self-defeating. For example, you may think that you're a poor speaker or group leader or interviewee or that you have to be perfect. Instead of thinking in terms of these unrealistic and self-defeating assumptions, substitute realistic ones, especially when tackling new communication situations.

Positive and supportive thoughts will help you restructure your thinking. Remind yourself of your successes, strengths, and virtues. Concentrate on your potential, not on your limitations. Use self-affirmations such as "I'm friendly and can communicate this," "I can learn the techniques for controlling my fear," "I'm a competent person and have the potential to be effective," "I can make mistakes and can learn from them," "I'm flexible and can adjust to different communication situations."

- **Practice performance visualization.** A variation of cognitive restructuring is performance visualization, a technique designed specifically to reduce the outward signs of apprehension and also to reduce the negative thinking that often creates anxiety.

  First, develop a positive attitude and a positive self-perception. Visualize yourself in the role of the effective communicator. Visualize yourself walking to the front of the room or into the interview fully and totally confident, fully in control of the situation. If a public speaking situation, visualize the audience in rapt attention and, as you finish, bursting into wild applause. Throughout this visualization, avoid all negative thoughts. As you visualize yourself, take note of how you walk, sit, position yourself, handle any notes, and respond to questions.

Second, model your performance on that of especially effective communicators. You see them all the time on television. YouTube makes these easy to access and enjoyable tow atch. As you view them gradually shift yourself into the role of speaker; become this speaker you admire.

- **Desensitize yourself.** Systematic desensitization is a technique for dealing with a variety of fears, including those involved in communication apprehension. The general idea is to create a hierarchy of behaviors leading up to the desired-but-feared behavior (say, speaking before an audience). One specific hierarchy might look like this:

5. Giving a speech in class
4. Introducing another speaker to the class
3. Speaking in a group in front of the class
2. Answering a question in class
1. Asking a question in class

The main objective of this experience is to learn to relax, beginning with relatively easy tasks and progressing to the behavior you're apprehensive about—in this case giving a speech in class. You begin at the bottom of the hierarchy and rehearse the first behavior mentally over a period of days until you can clearly visualize asking a question in class without any uncomfortable anxiety. Once you can accomplish this, move to the second level. Here you visualize a somewhat more threatening behavior; say, answering a question. Once you can do this, move to the third level, and so on until you get to the desired behavior.

In creating your hierarchy, use small steps to help you get from one step to the next more easily. Each success will make the next step easier. You might then go on to engage in the actual behaviors after you have comfortably visualized them: ask a question, answer a question, and so on.

Try It

The next time you anticipate a communication event that will create anxiety, try one of these strategies. For example, an easy one is to use visualization and try to see the new communication situation (the interview, the public speech) as conversation, perhaps conversation with a friend.

Strategies for

Argumentativeness

Contrary to popular usage, the term *argumentativeness* refers to a quality to be cultivated rather than avoided. Argumentativeness is your willingness to argue for a point of view, your tendency to speak your mind on significant issues. It's the preferred alternative to verbal aggressiveness which refers to a strategy that seeks to win an argument by inflicting psychological pain, by attacking the other person's self-concept.

Argumentativeness is constructive; the outcomes are positive in a variety of communication situations (interpersonal, group, organizational, family, and intercultural). Verbal aggressiveness, on the other hand, is destructive; the outcomes are negative in a variety of communication situations (interpersonal, group, organizational, family, and intercultural). Argumentativeness leads to relationship satisfaction. Aggressiveness leads to relationship dissatisfaction, not surprising for a strategy that aims to attack another's self-concept.

The Payoffs of Argumentativeness

There are a variety of payoffs/benefits/values to be gained from argumentativeness, especially when opposed to verbal aggressiveness. Argumentativeness, for example, may prevent relationship violence especially in domestic

Strategies for

Assertiveness

If you disagree with other people in a group, do you speak your mind? Do you allow others to take advantage of you because you're reluctant to say what you want? Do you feel uncomfortable when you have to state your opinion in a group? Questions such as these speak to your degree of assertiveness. If you want to get a start measuring your own assertiveness see the & Box, How Assertive Are You?

&

How Assertive Are You?

Respond instinctively rather than in the way you feel you should respond. Use the following scale: 5 = always or almost always true; 4 = usually true; 3 = sometimes true, sometimes false; 2 = usually false; and 1 = always or almost always false.

______ 1. I would express my opinion in a group even if my view contradicted the opinions of others.

______ 2. When asked to do something that I really don't want to do, I can say no without feeling guilty.

______ 3. I can express my opinion to my superiors on the job.

______ 4. I can start up a conversation with a stranger on a bus or at a business gathering without fear.

______ 5. I voice objection to people's behavior if I feel it infringes on my rights.

All five items in this test identified characteristics of assertive communication. So high scores (say about 20 and above) would indicate a high level of assertiveness. Low scores (say about 10 and below) would indicate a low level of assertiveness.

Assertive people operate with an "I win, you win" philosophy; they assume that both parties can gain something from an interpersonal interaction, even from a confrontation. Assertive people are more positive and score lower on measures of hopelessness than do nonassertive people. Assertive people are willing to assert their own rights. Unlike their aggressive counterparts, however, they don't hurt others in the process. Assertive people speak their minds and welcome others doing likewise.

Do realize that as with many other aspects of communication, there will be wide cultural differences when it comes to assertiveness. Assertiveness will be valued more by those cultures that stress competition, individual success, and independence. It will be valued much less by those cultures that stress cooperation, group success, and the interdependence of all members on one another. American students, for example, are found to be significantly more assertive than Japanese or Korean students. Thus, for some situations, assertiveness may be an effective strategy in one culture but may create problems in another. Assertiveness with an elder in many Asian and

Hispanic cultures, for example, may be seen as insulting and disrespectful.

Most people are nonassertive in certain situations. If you're one of these people and if you wish to increase your assertiveness, consider the following strategies:

- **Analyze assertive communications.** The first step in increasing your assertiveness is to understand the nature of assertive communications. Observe and analyze the messages of others. Learn to distinguish the differences among assertive and nonassertive messages. Focus on what makes one behavior assertive and another behavior nonassertive. After you've gained some skills in observing the behaviors of others, turn your analysis to yourself. Analyze situations in which you're normally assertive and situations in which you're more likely to act nonassertively. What characterizes these situations? What do the situations in which you're normally assertive have in common? How do you speak? How do you communicate nonverbally?

- **Rehearse assertive communications.** One way to rehearse assertiveness is to use desensitization techniques (see the chapter on Apprehension for more on this technique). Here you begin by visualizing a situation in which you're normally nonassertive. Then you build a hierarchy that begins with a relatively nonthreatening message and ends with the desired communication. For example, let's say that you have difficulty voicing your opinion to your supervisor at work. The desired behavior, then, is to tell your supervisor your opinions. To desensitize yourself, construct a hierarchy of visualized situations leading up to this desired behavior. Such a hierarchy might begin with visualizing yourself talking with your boss. Visualize this scenario until you can do it without any anxiety or discomfort. Once you have mastered this visualization, visualize a step closer to your goal, such as walking into your boss's office. Again, do this until your visualization creates no discomfort. Continue with these successive visualizations until you can visualize yourself telling your boss your opinion. As with the other visualizations, do this until you can do it while totally relaxed. This is the mental rehearsal. You might add a vocal dimension to this by actually acting out (with voice and gesture) telling your boss your opinion. Again, do this until you experience no difficulty or discomfort. Next, try doing this in front of a trusted and supportive friend or group of friends. Ideally this interaction will provide you with useful feedback. After this rehearsal, you're probably ready for the next step.

- **Communicate assertively.** This step is naturally the most difficult but obviously the most important. Here's a generally effective pattern to follow in communicating assertively:
  1. Describe the problem; don't evaluate or judge it. "We're all working on this advertising project together. You're missing half our meetings, and you still haven't produced your first report." Avoid messages that accuse or blame the other person.
  2. State how this problem affects you; tell the person how you feel. "My job depends on the success of this project, and I don't think it's fair that I have to do extra work to make up for what you're not doing."
  3. Propose solutions that are workable and that allow the person to save face. Describe or visualize the situation if your solution were put into effect. "If you can get your report to the group by Tuesday, we'll still be able to meet our deadline. I could give you a call on Monday to remind you."
  4. Confirm understanding. "It's clear that we can't produce this project if you're not going to pull

your own weight. Will you have the report to us by Tuesday?"

Keep in mind that assertiveness is not always the most desirable communication pattern. Assertive people are assertive when they want to be, but they can be nonassertive if the situation calls for it. For example, you might wish to be nonassertive in a situation in which assertiveness might emotionally hurt the other person. Let's say that an older relative wishes you to do something for her or him. You could assert your rights and say no, but in doing so you would probably hurt this person; it might be better simply to do as asked.

Try It

As you try to increase your assertiveness, a note of caution should be added. It's easy to visualize a situation in which, for example, people are talking behind you in a movie, and with your newfound enthusiasm for assertiveness, you tell them to be quiet. It's also easy to see yourself getting smashed in the teeth as a result. In applying the principles of assertive communication, be careful that you don't go beyond what you can handle effectively.

Strategies for

Attractiveness

Everyone wants to be thought attractive to others as well as to oneself and we all spend considerable time making ourselves more attractive. And of course the attractiveness of others will influence how we respond to them; we want to interact with people we find attractive.

If you're like most people, then you're attracted to others on the basis of a variety of factors: similarity, proximity, reinforcement, physical attractiveness and personality, and reciprocity of liking. Each of these suggests a simple strategy:

- **Express similarities.** People like people and are attracted to those who are like them, who have similar attitudes and beliefs. So, emphasize the similarities and play down the differences. If you could construct your mate, according to the similarity principle, it's likely that your mate would look, act, and think very much like you. Generally, people like those who are similar to them in nationality, race, abilities, physical characteristics, intelligence, and attitudes. And we generally date and mate those who are similar to us in attractiveness. That is, you select persons for dating and ultimately mating who are neither much more attractive nor much less attractive than you are. It's referred to as the matching hypothesis.

- **Keep in touch.** Allow the proximity principle to operate. Social media have made this extremely easy and keeping in touch is now intermeshed with most people's interactional lives. Proximity increases attraction. If you look around at people you find attractive, you'll probably find that they're people who live or work close to you. Proximity, or physical closeness, is most important in the early stages of interaction—for example, during the first days of school (in class or in dormitories). The importance of proximity as a factor in attraction decreases, though always remaining significant, as the opportunity to interact with more distant others increases.

- **Reinforce**. We enjoy being complimented, supported, thought highly of. We're attracted to people who reward us, who give us things—whether social or material. Reinforcement increases attraction. Not surprisingly, you're attracted to people who give rewards, which can range from a simple compliment to an expensive cruise. You're also attracted to people you reward. That is, you come to like people for whom you do favors; for example, you've probably increased your liking for persons after buying them an expensive present or going out of your way to do them a special favor. In these situations you justify your behavior by believing that the person was worth your efforts; otherwise, you'd have to admit to spending effort or money on people who don't deserve it.

- **Increase your physical and personality attractiveness.** There are many things you can do here—comb your hair, wear becoming clothes, and focus on the other person, for example. Physical and personality factors increase attraction. One of the factors accounting for attractiveness is symmetry—symmetrical faces seem to be considered attractive in all cultures. Another factor is a mixture of youthfulness and sexual maturity that is revealed mainly in the face. Additionally, you probably tend to like people who have a pleasant rather than an unpleasant personality (although people will differ on what is and what is not an attractive personality).

- **Be liking.** If you like someone and express this liking in appropriate ways, you're likely to be thought more attractive and to be liked more. Reciprocity of liking increases attraction. It will come as no surprise that research supports what you already know from your own experience: you tend to be attracted to people you think are attracted to you; you come to like those who you think like you. This tendency, also known as *reciprocity of attraction* or *reciprocal liking*, is seen in a variety of situations. You initiate potential friendships and romantic relationships with people who you think will like you, certainly not with those you think dislike you. There is even evidence to show that people like "likers"—people who like others generally—more than they like people who don't express such liking.

In addition to these five general strategies of increasing attractiveness, there are a variety of specific strategies that are likely to get you perceived as more attractive. Here are some dos and don'ts:

- **Accommodate.** Accommodate or adjust to the communication style of the other person if you want to increase your attractiveness. When you accommodate, you imitate the speaking style of the other person. Usually, this is effective when it's done to a small degree and goes unnoticed on a conscious level. If done too much, it may appear as mocking and insulting.

- **Gesture**. Gesture to show liveliness and animation in ways that are appropriate to the situation and to the message. But, don't gesture for the sake of gesturing or gesture in ways that may prove offensive to members of other cultures.

- **Nod and lean forward**. This helps you to signal that you're listening and are interested. But, avoid going on automatic pilot, nodding without any coordination with what is being said or lean forward so much that you intrude on the other's space.

- **Express positive attitudes; smile.** Show your interest, attention, and positiveness verbally and facially. But, be careful that you don't overdo it; inappropriate smiling, for example, is likely to be perceived negatively.

- **Make eye contact in moderation.** Don't stare, ogle, glare, or otherwise make the person feel that he or she is under scrutiny. Be sure to respond in kind to another's eyebrow flash (raising the eyebrow as a way of acknowledging another person).

- **Touch in moderation when appropriate**. Avoid touching excessively or too intimately. When it doubt, avoid touching another.

- **Use vocal variation.** Vary your rate, rhythm, pitch, and volume to communicate your animation and involvement in what you're saying. But, don't fall into the pattern where, for example, your voice goes up and down, up and down, up and down without any relationship to what you're saying.

- **Use silence**. Listen for at least the same amount of time as you speak. Show that you're listening with appropriate facial reactions, posture, and other verbal and nonverbal cues that say "I'm listening." Avoid listening motionlessly or in ways that suggest you're only listening half-heartedly.

- **Establish physical closeness.** Stand reasonably close to show a connectedness. But, be careful that you don't exceed the other person's comfort zone. Stand and sit tall; don't slouch.

- **Present a pleasant smell**. Be careful to camouflage the onions, garlic, or smoke that you're so used to. Avoid overdoing the cologne or perfume or wearing your body sweat as a sign of a heavy workout.

- **Dress appropriately to the situation**. Avoid clothing that proves uncomfortable or that calls attention to itself and hence away from your message.

Try It

The next time you want to increase your attractiveness—whether at a club or in the workplace—try one or two of the strategies. For example, in the next conversation try to be especially positive, you don't have to lie here; just focus on the positive. Or touch the other person gently on the hand or shoulder.

Strategies for

Complimenting

A compliment is a message of praise, flattery, or congratulations. It's the opposite of criticism, insult, or complaint. It can be expressed in face-to-face interaction or on social media sites when, for example, you retweet someone or indicate "like" or "+1" or when you comment on a blog post. The compliment functions like a kind of interpersonal glue; it's a way a relating to another person with positiveness. It's also a conversation starter, "I like your watch; may I ask where you got it?" In online communication—when you poke, tag, +1, or retweet, for example, it's a reminder that you're thinking of someone (and being complimentary). Another purpose the compliment serves is to encourage the other person to compliment you—even if not immediately (which often seems inappropriate).

Yet compliments are sometimes difficult to express and even more difficult to respond to without discomfort or embarrassment. Fortunately, there are easy-to-follow strategies for giving a compliment:

- **Be real and honest.** Say what you mean and omit giving compliments you don't believe in. They'll likely sound insincere and won't serve any useful purpose.

- **Compliment in moderation.** A compliment that is too extreme (say, for example, "that's the best decorated apartment I've ever seen in my life") may be viewed as dishonest. Similarly, don't compliment at every possible occasion; if you do, your compliments will seem too easy to win and not really meaningful.

- **Be totally complimentary.** Avoid qualifying your compliments. If you hear yourself giving a compliment and then adding a "but" or a "however," be careful; you're likely going to qualify your compliment. Unfortunately, in such situations, many people will remember the qualification rather than the compliment, and the entire compliment + qualification will appear as a criticism. Especially avoid the backhanded compliment; see the & Box.

The Backhanded Compliment

A backhanded compliment is really not a compliment at all; it's usually an insult masquerading as a compliment. For example, you might give a backhanded compliment if you say "That's a beautiful red sweater; it takes away from your pale complexion and makes you look less washed out" (it compliments the sweater but criticizes the person's complexion) or "Looks like you've finally lost a few pounds, am I right?" (it compliments a slimmer appearance but points out the person's being overweight).

- **Be specific.** Direct your compliment at something specific rather than something general. Instead of saying something general, such as *I like your design*, you might say something more specific, such as *I like your design; the colors and fonts are perfect.*

- **Be personal in your own feelings.** For example, say *Your song really moved me; it made me recall so many good* *times.* At the same time, avoid any compliment that can be misinterpreted as overly sexual.

The other half of complimenting, of course, is receiving it, not as easy to do gracefully as it may at first seem. In receiving a compliment, people generally take either one of two options: denial or acceptance. Many people simply deny the compliment ("It's nice of you to say, but I know I was terrible"), some minimize it ("It isn't like I wrote the great American novel; it was just an article that no one will read"), some change the subject ("So, where should we go for dinner?"), and still others say nothing. Each of these responses creates problems. When you deny the legitimacy of the compliment, you're saying that the person isn't being sincere or doesn't know what he or she is talking about. When you minimize it, you say, in effect, that the person doesn't understand what you've done or what he or she is complimenting. When you change the subject or say nothing, again, you're saying, in effect, that the compliment isn't having any effect; you're ignoring it because it isn't meaningful.

Accepting the compliment seems the much better alternative. In accepting, consider these strategies:

- **Smile with eye contact.** Avoid looking at the floor or at other people. Focus on the person giving you the compliment.
- **Say a simple "thank you."** And say it as you mean it; don't throw it away, as if it doesn't matter to you.
- **Include a personal reflection.** If appropriate, you might include a personal reflection where you explain (very briefly) the meaning of the compliment and why it's important to you. For example, you might say: "I really appreciate your comments; I worked hard on that design, and it's great to hear it was effective.").

Try It

Try complimenting someone for something he or she accomplished. Craft your compliment before saying it—at least at the early stages of learning to compliment; don't try to develop an effective compliment without thinking it through, especially if this is a work situation. And, the next time someone compliments you, accept it graciously.

Strategies for

Conflict Management

Conflict is disagreement between or among interdependent individuals (for example, friends, lovers, family members) who perceive their goals as incompatible. More specifically, conflict occurs when people:

- are interdependent (they're connected in some significant way); what one person does has an effect on the other person.
- are mutually aware of incompatible goals. A conflict situation exists if the achievement of one person's goal means the failure of the other person's goal. For example, if one person wants to buy a new car and the other person wants to pay down the mortgage (with their unexpected bonus), there is conflict. Note that this situation would not pose a conflict if the couple had unlimited resources, in which case, they could both buy the car and pay down the mortgage; their goals would not be incompatible.
- perceive each other as interfering with the attainment of their own goals. For example, you may want to study but your roommate may want to party; the attainment of either goal would interfere with the attainment of the other goal.

Among the implications of this concept of interdependency is that the greater the interdependency, the greater the number of issues about which conflict can center and the greater the impact of the conflict on the individuals and on the relationship. Put differently, when you're in a close relationship, you're likely to argue about more things than would be the case with more distant acquaintances. Also, and this is especially important, the closer the relationship, the more important conflict and its resolution becomes. Looked at in this way, it's easy to appreciate how important understanding conflict and the strategies of effective conflict management are to your relationship life.

- **Set the stage.** First, try to fight in private. When you air your conflicts in front of others, you create a variety of other problems. You may not be willing to be totally honest when third parties are present; you may feel you have to save face and therefore must win the fight at all costs. This may lead you to use strategies to win the argument rather than to resolve the conflict. You may become so absorbed by the image that others will have of you that you forget you have a relationship problem that needs to be resolved. Also, you run the risk of embarrassing your partner in front of others, and this embarrassment may create resentment and hostility.

  Be sure you're each ready to fight. Although conflicts arise at the most inopportune times, you can choose the time to resolve them. Confronting your partner when she or he comes home after a hard day of work may not be the right time for resolving a conflict. Make sure you're both relatively free of other problems and ready to deal with the conflict at hand.

  Know what you're fighting about. Sometimes people in a relationship become so hurt and angry that they lash out at the other person just to vent their own frustration. The problem at the center of the conflict (for example, the uncapped toothpaste tube) is merely an excuse to express anger. Any attempt to resolve this "problem" will be doomed to failure, because the problem addressed is not what is causing the conflict. Instead, the underlying hostility, anger, and frustration need to be addressed.

Fight about problems that can be solved. Fighting about past behaviors or about family members or situations over which you have no control solves nothing; instead, it creates additional difficulties. Any attempt at resolution will fail, because the problems are incapable of being solved. Often such conflicts are concealed attempts at expressing frustration or dissatisfaction.

- **Define the conflict.** Usually, the nature of the conflict is clear to the individuals. But, when it might not be or when there might be different opinions then a more detailed definition needs to be undertaken. See the & Box, Defining the Conflict, for some ways this analysis might be accomplished.

Defining the Conflict

Here are five strategies for defining a conflict in ways that can help lead to the conflict's peaceful resolution.

- **Define both content and relationship issues.** Define the obvious content issues (who should do the dishes, who should take the kids to school) as well as the underlying relationship issues (who has been avoiding household responsibilities, whose time is more valuable).
- **Define the problem in specific terms.** Conflict defined in the abstract is difficult to deal with and resolve. It's one thing for a husband to say that his wife is "cold and unfeeling" and quite another to say that she does not call him at the office, kiss him when he comes home, or hold his hand when they're at a party. These behaviors can be agreed on and dealt with, but the abstract "cold and unfeeling" remains elusive.

- **Focus on the present.** Avoid gunnysacking (a term derived from the large burlap bag called a gunnysack)—the practice of storing up grievances so they may be unloaded at another time. Often, when one person gunnysacks, the other person gunnysacks; for example, the birthdays you forgot and the times you arrived late for dinner are all thrown at you. The result is two people dumping their stored-up grievances on each other with no real attention to the present problem.
- **Empathize.** Try to understand the nature of the conflict from the other person's point of view. Why is your partner disturbed that you're not doing the dishes? Why is your neighbor complaining about taking the kids to school? Once you have empathically understood the other person's feelings, validate those feelings when appropriate. If your partner is hurt or angry and you believe such feelings are legitimate and justified, say so: "You have a right to be angry; I shouldn't have said what I did about your mother. I'm sorry. But I still don't want to go on vacation with her." In expressing validation, you're not necessarily expressing agreement; you're merely stating that your partner has feelings that you recognize as legitimate.
- **Avoid mind reading.** Don't try to read the other person's mind. Ask questions to make sure you understand the problem as the other person is experiencing it. Ask directly and simply: "Why are you insisting that I take the dog out now, when I have to call three clients before nine o'clock?"

- **Examine possible solutions.** Most conflicts can probably be resolved through a variety of solutions. Here are a few suggestions. Brainstorm by yourself or with your partner.

Try not to inhibit or censor yourself or your partner as you generate these potential solutions. Once you have proposed a variety of solutions, look especially for solutions that will enable each party to win—to get something he or she wants. Avoid win–lose solutions, in which one person wins and one loses. Such outcomes will cause difficulty for the relationship by engendering frustration and resentment. Carefully weigh the costs and the rewards that each solution entails. Most solutions will involve costs to one or both parties. Seek solutions in which the costs and the rewards will be evenly shared.

Using a specific example will help us work through the various steps in the conflict resolution process. In this example, the conflict revolves around Pat's not wanting to socialize with Chris's friends. Chris is devoted to these friends, but Pat actively dislikes them. Chris thinks they're wonderful and exciting; Pat thinks they're unpleasant and boring.

For example, among the solutions that Pat and Chris might identify are these:

1. Chris should not interact with these friends anymore.
2. Pat should interact with Chris's friends.
3. Chris should see these friends without Pat.

Clearly solutions 1 and 2 are win–lose solutions. In solution 1, Pat wins and Chris loses; in 2, Chris wins and Pat loses. Solution 3 has some possibilities. Both might win and neither must necessarily lose. This potential solution, then, needs to be looked at more closely.

- **Test the solution.** First, test the solution mentally. How does it feel now? How will it feel tomorrow? Are you comfortable with it? In our example, will Pat be comfortable with Chris's socializing with these friends alone? Some of Chris's friends are attractive; will this cause difficulty for Pat and Chris's relationship? Will Chris give people too much to gossip about? Will Chris feel guilty? Will Chris enjoy seeing these friends without Pat?

Second, test the solution in practice. Put the solution into operation. How does it work? If it doesn't work, then discard it and try another solution. Give each solution a fair chance, but don't hang on to a solution when it's clear that it won't resolve the conflict.

Perhaps Chris might go out without Pat once to test this solution. Afterward, the couple can evaluate the experiment. Did the friends think there was something wrong with Chris's relationship with Pat? Did Chris feel guilty? Did Chris enjoy this new experience? How did Pat feel? Did Pat feel jealous? Lonely? Abandoned?

- **Evaluate the solution.** Did the solution help resolve the conflict? Is the situation better now than it was before the solution was tried? Share your feelings and evaluations of the solution. Pat and Chris now need to share their perceptions of this possible solution. Would they be comfortable with this solution on a monthly basis? Is the solution worth the costs each will pay? Are the costs and rewards evenly distributed? Might other solutions be more effective? An interesting way to analyze a problem is provided in the & Box, The Six Thinking Hats.

The Six Thinking Hats

In analyzing problems try using the six "thinking hats" as a way of seeking different perspectives. With each hat you look at the problem from a different angle.

- **The fact hat** focuses attention on the facts and figures that bear on the problem. For example, how can Pat learn more about the rewards that Chris gets from the friends? How can Chris learn why Pat doesn't like these great friends?
- **The feeling hat** focuses attention on the emotional responses to the problem. How does Pat feel when Chris goes out with these friends? How does Chris feel when Pat refuses to meet them?
- **The negative argument hat** asks you to become the devil's advocate. How may this relationship deteriorate if Chris continues seeing these friends without Pat or if Pat resists interacting with Chris's friends?
- **The positive benefits hat** asks you to look at the upside. What are the opportunities that Chris's seeing friends without Pat might yield? What benefits might Pat and Chris get from this new arrangement?
- **The creative new idea hat** focuses on new ways of looking at the problem. In what other ways can Pat and Chris look at this problem? What other possible solutions might they consider?

- **The control of thinking hat** helps you analyze what you're doing; it asks you to reflect on your own thinking. Have Pat and Chris adequately defined the problem? Are they focusing too much on insignificant issues? Have they given enough attention to possible negative effects?

- **Accept or reject the solution.** If you accept the solution, you're ready to put it into more permanent operation. Let's say that Pat is actually quite happy with the solution. Pat was able to use the evening to visit college friends. The next time Chris goes out with the friends Pat doesn't like, Pat intends to go out with some friends from college. Chris feels pretty good about seeing friends without Pat. Chris explains that they have both decided to see their friends separately and both are comfortable with this decision. If, however, either Pat or Chris feels unhappy with this solution, they will have to try out another solution or perhaps go back and redefine the problem and seek other ways to resolve it.

- **Wrap it up.** Even after the conflict is resolved, there is still work to be done. Often, after one conflict is supposedly settled, another conflict will emerge—because, for example, one person feels that he or she has been harmed and needs to retaliate and take revenge in order to restore a sense of self-worth. So it's especially important that the conflict be resolved and not be allowed to generate other, perhaps more significant conflicts. Learn from the conflict and from the process you went through in trying to resolve it. For example, can you identify the fight strategies that merely aggravated the situation? Do you or your partner need a cooling-off period? Can you tell when minor issues are going to escalate into major arguments? Does avoidance make matters worse? What issues are particularly disturbing and likely to cause difficulties? Can they be avoided?

Keep the conflict in perspective. Be careful not to blow it out of proportion to the extent that you begin to define your relationship in terms of conflict. Avoid the tendency to see disagreement as inevitably leading to major blowups. Conflicts in most relationships actually occupy a very small percentage of the couple's time, and yet in recollection they often loom extremely large.

Attack your negative feelings. Most often such feelings arise because one or both parties used unfair fight strategies to undermine the other person—for example, personal rejection, manipulation, or force. Resolve to avoid such unfair tactics in the future, but at the same time let go of guilt and blame toward yourself and your partner. Apologize for anything you did wrong. Your partner should do likewise; after all, both parties are usually responsible for the conflict.

Increase the exchange of rewards and cherishing behaviors to demonstrate your positive feelings and to show you're over the conflict and want the relationship to survive and flourish.

Try It

Review a recent conflict and try to identify the various stages noted here. Did you follow the strategies identified here? Would they have helped?

Strategies for

Conversational Closings

The closing of a conversation is the goodbye, which often reveals how satisfied the persons were with the conversation: "I hope you'll call soon" or "Don't call us, we'll call you." The closing also may be used to schedule future conversations: "Give me a call tomorrow night" or "Let's meet for lunch at twelve." When closings are indefinite or vague, conversation often becomes awkward; you're not quite sure if you should say goodbye or if you should wait for something else to be said.

Closing a conversation can be an awkward and uncomfortable part of an interaction. Here are a few strategies you might consider. See the & Box, E-Mail Closings, for ways of closing an e-mail exchange.

&

E-Mail Closings

Closing a conversation in e-mail follows the same principles as closing a face-to-face conversation. But exactly when you end the e-mail exchange is often not clear, partly because the absence of nonverbal cues creates ambiguity. For example, if you ask someone a question and the other person answers, do you then e-mail again and say "thanks"? If so, should the other person e-mail you back and say, "It was my pleasure"? And, if so, should you then e-mail back and say, "I appreciate your willingness to answer my questions"? And, if so, should the other person then respond with something like "It was no problem"?

On the one hand, you don't want to prolong the interaction more than necessary; on the other, you don't want to appear impolite. So how do you signal (politely) that the e-mail exchange should stop? Here are a few suggestions:

- Include in your e-mail the notation NRN (No Reply Necessary).
- If you're replying with information the other person requested, end your message with something like "I hope this helps."
- Title or head your message FYI (For Your Information), indicating that your message is just to keep someone in the loop.
- When you make a request for information, end your message with "thank you in advance."

- **Reflect back on the conversation.** For example, you might briefly summarize it so as to bring it to a close. For example: "I'm glad I ran into you and found out what happened at that union meeting. I'll probably be seeing you at the meetings next week."

- **Be direct.** Directly state the desire to end the conversation and to get on with other things. For example: "I'd like to continue talking, but I really have to run. I'll see you around."

- **Refer to future interaction.** For example: "Why don't we get together next week sometime and continue this discussion?"

- **Ask for closure.** For example: "Have I explained what you wanted to know?"

- **Express your enjoyment of the interaction.** For example: "I really enjoyed talking with you."

With any of these closings, it should be clear to the other person that you're attempting to end the conversation. Obviously, you will have to use more direct methods with those who don't take these subtle hints or don't realize that both persons are responsible for the interaction and for bringing it to a satisfactory close.

Try It

The next time you're in a conversation and you want to end it, try one of these strategies. You're likely to find that some strategies work better on some people and other strategies work better on others.

Strategies for

Conversational Openings

The first step in conversation is to open it. Usually you open a conversation with some kind of greeting: A "Hi. How are you?" or "Hello, this is Joe" or a poke on Facebook. The greeting is a good example of a message that establishes a connection between two people and opens up the channels for more meaningful interaction. When you send a friend a photo of strawberry cheesecake or a virtual gift, you're creating an opportunity for communication; you're saying that you're thinking of the person and want to communicate. A simple tweet or post likewise can serve as a conversation opener. Openings, of course, may be nonverbal as well as verbal. A smile, kiss, or handshake may be as clear an opening as "Hello." Greetings are so common that they often go unnoticed. But when they're omitted—as when the doctor begins the conversation by saying, "What's wrong?"—you may feel uncomfortable and thrown off guard.

In normal conversation, the greeting is reciprocated with a greeting similar in degree of formality and intensity. When it isn't—when the other person turns away or responds coldly to your friendly "Good morning"—you know that something is wrong.

Openings are also generally consistent in tone with the main part of the conversation; a cheery "How ya doing today, bud?" is not normally followed by news of a family death; and a friendly conversation is not begun with insensitive openers: "Wow, you've gained a few pounds haven't you?"

Several strategies to opening a conversation can be derived from the elements of the communication process:

- **Use self-references.** Say something about yourself. Such references may be of the "name, rank, and serial number" type—for example: "My name is Joe. I'm from Omaha." On the first day of class, students might say, "I'm worried about this class" or "I took this instructor last semester; she was excellent."

- **Refer to the other person.** Say something about the other person or ask a question: "I like that sweater." "Didn't we meet at Charlie's?" Of course, there are pitfalls here. But avoid commenting comment on the person's race ("My uncle married a Korean"), the person's affectional orientation ("Nice to meet you; I have a gay brother"), or physical disability ("It must be awful to be so limited").

- **Refer to the relationship.** Say something about the two of you: for example, "May I buy you a coffee?" "Would you like to dance?" or simply "May I join you?"

- **Make reference to the context.** Say something about the physical, social–psychological, cultural, or temporal context. The familiar "Do you have the time?" is a reference of this type. But you can be more creative and say, for example, "This restaurant seems very friendly" or "This painting is fantastic."

Another way of looking at the process of initiating conversations is to examine the infamous "opening line," the opener designed to begin a romantic relationship. On this see the & Box, The Opening Line.

The Opening Line

Consider your own opening lines (or the opening lines that have been used on you). Let's say you're at a club and want to strike up a conversation—and perhaps spark a relationship. Which of the following are you most likely to use?

- Cute–flippant openers are humorous, indirect, and ambiguous as to whether or not the person opening the conversation really wants an extended encounter. Examples: "Is that really your hair?" "I bet the cherries jubilee isn't as sweet as you are."
- Innocuous openers are highly ambiguous as to whether these are simple comments that might be made to just anyone or whether they're in fact openers designed to initiate an extended encounter. Examples: "What do you think of the band?" "Could you show me how to work this machine?"
- Direct openers demonstrate clearly the speaker's interest in meeting the other person. Examples: "I feel a little embarrassed about this, but I'd like to meet you." "Would you like to have coffee after dinner?"

One advantage of cute-flippant openers is that they're indirect enough to cushion any rejection. These are also, however, the lines least preferred by both men and women. In contrast, both men and women generally like innocuous openers; they're indirect enough to allow for an easy out if the other person doesn't want to talk. On direct openers, however, genders differ. Men like direct openers that are very clear in meaning, possibly because men are not used to having another person initiate a meeting. Women prefer openers that aren't too strong and that are relatively modest.

As you know from experience, conversations are most satisfying when they're upbeat and positive. So it's generally best to lead off with something positive rather than something negative. Say, for example, "I like the music here" instead of "Don't you just hate this place?" Also, it's best not to be too revealing; disclosing too much too early in an interaction can make the other person feel uncomfortable.

Try It

The next time you're in a position to initiate conversation, consider using some of these strategies. The cardinal rule is positiveness. Even if you stumble and you're positive, you'll probably be successful.

Strategies for

Conversational Cooperation

During conversation you probably follow the principle of cooperation; you and the other person implicitly agree to cooperate in trying to understand what each is saying. You cooperate largely by using four conversational maxims—principles that speakers and listeners in the United States and in many other cultures follow in conversation. Although the names for these maxims may be new, the strategies themselves will be easily recognized.

- **Follow the maxim of quantity.** Be as informative as necessary to communicate the intended meaning. Thus, in keeping with the quantity maxim, you include information that makes the meaning clear but omit what does not; you give neither too little nor too much information. You see people violate this maxim when they try to relate an incident and digress to give unnecessary information. You find yourself thinking or saying, "Get to the point; so what happened?" This maxim is also violated when necessary information is omitted. In this situation, you find yourself constantly interrupting to ask questions: "Where were they?" "When did this happen?" "Who else was there?" For some of the ways this maxim is violated in e-communication, see the & Box, Maxim of Quantity Violations.

Maxim of Quantity Violations

This simple maxim is frequently violated in e-mail communication. Here, for example, are three ways in which e-mail often violates the maxim of quantity and some suggestions on how to avoid these violations.

- Chain e-mails (and "forwards" of jokes or pictures) often violate the maxim of quantity by sending people information they don't really need or want. Some people maintain lists of e-mail addresses and send all these people the same information. It's highly unlikely that everyone on these lists will need or want to read the long list of jokes you find so funny. Suggestion: Avoid chain e-mail (at least most of the time). When something comes along that you think someone you know would like to read, send it on to the specific one, two, or three people you know would like to receive it.
- When chain e-mails are used, they often contain the e-mail addresses of everyone on the chain. These extensive headers clog the system and also reveal e-mail addresses that some people may prefer to keep private or to share with others at their own discretion. Suggestion: When you do send chain e-mails (and in some situations, they serve useful purposes), conceal the e-mail addresses of your recipients by using some general description such as "undisclosed recipients."

- Large attachments take time to download and can create problems for people who do not have the latest technology. Not everyone wants to see the two hundred photos of your last vacation. Suggestion: Use attachments in moderation; find out first who would like to receive photos and who would not.

- **Follow the maxim of quality.** Say what you know or assume to be true, and do not say what you know to be false. When you're in conversation, you assume that the other person's information is true—at least as far as he or she knows. When you speak with people who frequently violate the quality maxim by lying, exaggerating, or minimizing major problems, you come to distrust what such individuals are saying and wonder what is true and what is fabricated.

- **Follow the maxim of relation.** Talk about what is relevant to the conversation. Thus, the relation maxim states, if you're talking about Pat and Chris and say, for example, "Money causes all sorts of relationship problems," it's assumed by others that your comment is somehow related to Pat and Chris. This principle is frequently violated by speakers who digress widely or frequently interject irrelevant comments, causing you to wonder how these comments are related to what you're discussing.

- **Follow the maxim of manner.** Be clear, avoid ambiguities, be relatively brief, and organize your thoughts into a meaningful sequence. Thus, in accordance with the manner maxim, you use words that the listener understands and clarify words that you suspect the listener will not understand. When talking with a child, for example, you simplify your vocabulary. Similarly, you adjust your manner of speaking on the basis of the information you and the listener share. When talking to a close friend, for example, you can refer to mutual acquaintances and to experiences you've had together. When talking to a stranger, however, you'll either omit such references or explain them.

These four maxims aptly describe most conversations as they take place in much of the United States. Recognize, however, that maxims will vary from one culture to another. See the & Box, Cultural Maxims, for two cultural differences.

&

Cultural Maxims

Here are just two maxims to illustrate cultural differences.

- In Japanese conversations and group discussions, a maxim of preserving peaceful relationships with others may be observed. Thus, for example, it would be considered inappropriate to argue and to directly demonstrate that another person is wrong. It would be inappropriate to contribute to another person's embarrassment or, worse, loss of face.
- The maxim of self-denigration, observed in the conversations of Chinese speakers, may require that you avoid taking credit for some accomplishment or make less of some ability or talent you have. To put yourself down in this way is a form of politeness that seeks to elevate the person to whom you're speaking.

Try It

Reflect back on a recent conversation and examine it for the four maxims. Did you follow them? Did the other person follow them?

Strategies for

Critical Thinking

Critical thinking—the ability to think logically, sanely, objectively, rationally—is essential in personal and professional success. Here are six strategies for thinking and talking more critically. All of these come from General Semantics—the study of the relationships among language, thought, and behavior. Check out their website at www.generalsemantics.org. These six strategies will help you to more accurately align your language with the real world—the world of words and not words, infinite complexity, facts and inferences, sameness and difference, extremes and middle ground, and constant change.

- **Extensionalize.** The term *intensional orientation* (the "s" is intentional) refers to the tendency to view people, objects, and events in terms of how they're talked about or labeled rather than in terms of how they actually exist. *Ex*tensional orientation is the opposite: It's a tendency to look first at the actual people, objects, and events and then at the labels; it's the tendency to be guided by what you see happening rather than by the way something is talked about or labeled. *In*tensional orientation occurs when you act as if the words and labels were more important than the things they represent—as if the map were more important than the territory. In its extreme form, intensional orientation is seen in the person who is afraid of dogs and who begins to sweat when shown a picture of a dog or when hearing people talk about dogs. Here the person is responding to a label as if it were the actual thing. In its more common form, intensional orientation occurs when you see people through your preconceived ideas instead of on the basis of their specific behaviors. For example, it occurs when you think of a professor as an unworldly egghead—because that's your generalized image of a professor—before getting to know the specific professor.

The corrective to intensional orientation is to focus first on the object, person, or event and then on the way in which the object, person, or event is talked about. Labels are certainly helpful guides, but don't allow them to obscure what they're meant to symbolize.

- **Avoid allness.** The world is infinitely complex, and because of this you can never say all there is to say about anything—at least not logically. This is particularly true when you're dealing with people. You may think you know all there is to know about certain individuals or about why they did what they did, yet clearly you don't know all. You can never know all the reasons you yourself do something, so there is no way you can know all the reasons your parents, friends, or enemies did something. Suppose, for example, you go on a first date with someone who, at least during the first hour or so, turns out to be less interesting than you would have liked. Because of this initial impression, you may infer that this person is dull, always and everywhere. Yet it could be that this person is simply ill at ease or shy during first meetings. The problem here is that you run the risk of judging a person on the basis of a very short acquaintanceship. Further, if you then define this person as dull, you're likely to treat the person as dull and fulfill your own prophecy.

  A useful extensional device that can help you avoid allness is to end each statement, sometimes verbally but always mentally, with an "etc." (et cetera)—a reminder that there is more to learn, know, and say; every statement is inevitably incomplete. To be sure, some people overuse the "et cetera." They use it as a substitute for being specific, which defeats its purpose. Instead, it should be used to mentally remind yourself that there is more to know and more to say.

- **Avoid fact-inference confusion.** Language enables us to form statements of facts and inferences without making any linguistic distinction between the two. Similarly, when we listen to such statements, we often don't make a clear distinction between statements of facts and statements of inference. Yet there are great differences between the two. Barriers to clear thinking can be created when inferences are treated as facts, a hazard called fact–inference confusion. For example, you can make statements about things that you observe, and you can make statements about things that you have not observed. In form or structure these statements are similar; they cannot be distinguished from each other by any grammatical analysis. For example, you can say, "She's wearing a blue jacket" as well as "She's harboring an illogical hatred." If you diagrammed these sentences, they would yield identical structures, and yet you know that they're different types of statements. In the first sentence, you can observe the jacket and the blue color; the sentence constitutes a *factual statement*. But how do you observe "illogical hatred"? Obviously, this is not a descriptive statement but an *inferential statement*, a statement that you make not solely on the basis of what you observe but on the basis of what you observe plus your own conclusions.

  If you want to test your own ability to distinguish facts from inferences see the & Box, Facts and Inferences.

Facts and Inferences

Carefully read the following account, modeled on a report developed by William Haney and the observations based on it. Indicate whether you think the observations are true, false, or doubtful on the basis of the information presented in the report. Circle T if the observation is definitely true, F if the observation is definitely false, and ? if the observation may be either true or false. Judge each observation in order. Don't reread the observations after you have indicated your judgment, and don't change any of your answers.

A well-liked college teacher had just completed making up the final examinations and had turned off the lights in the office. Just then a tall, broad figure appeared and demanded the examination. The professor opened the drawer. Everything in the drawer was picked up and the individual ran down the corridor. The dean was notified immediately.

T F ? 1. The thief was tall and broad.
T F ? 2. The professor turned off the lights.
T F ? 3. A tall figure demanded the examination.
T F ? 4. The examination was picked up by someone.
T F ? 5. The examination was picked up by the professor.
T F ? 6. A tall figure appeared after the professor turned off the lights in the office.
T F ? 7. The man who opened the drawer was the professor.
T F ? 8. The professor ran down the corridor.
T F ? 9. The drawer was never actually opened.
T F ? 10. Three persons are referred to in this report.

This test is designed to trap you into making inferences and treating them as facts. Statement 3 is true (it's in the report); statement 9 is false (the drawer was opened); but all other statements are inferences and should have been marked "?". Review the remaining eight statements to see why you cannot be certain that any of them are either true or false.

Distinguishing between these two types of statements does not imply that one type is better than the other. Both types of statements are useful; both are important. The problem arises when you treat an inferential statement as if it were fact. Phrase your inferential statements as tentative. Recognize that such statements may be wrong. Leave open the possibility of other alternatives.

- **Avoid indiscrimination.** Nature seems to abhor sameness at least as much as vacuums, for nowhere in the universe can you find identical entities. Everything is unique. Language, however, provides common nouns, such as *teacher*, *student*, *friend*, *enemy*, *war*, *politician*, *liberal*, and the like, that may lead you to focus on similarities. Such nouns can lead you to group together all teachers, all students, and all friends and divert attention from the uniqueness of each individual, object, and event. The misevaluation known as indiscrimination—a form of stereotyping—occurs when you focus on classes of individuals, objects, or events and fail to see that each is unique and needs to be looked at individually. Indiscrimination can be seen in such statements as these:
    - He's just like the rest of them: lazy, stupid, a real slob.
    - I really don't want another ethnic on the board of directors. One is enough for me.
    - Read a romance novel? I read one when I was 16. That was enough to convince me.

A useful antidote to indiscrimination is the extensional device called the *index*, a mental subscript that identifies each individual in a group as an individual even though all members of the group may be covered by the same label. For example, when you think and talk of an individual politician as just a "politician," you may fail to see the uniqueness in this politician and the differences between this particular politician and other politicians. However, when you think with the index—when you think not of politician but of politician1 or politician2 or politician3—you're less likely to fall into the trap of indiscrimination and more likely to focus on the differences among politicians. The same is true with members of cultural, national, or religious groups; when you think of Iraqi1 and Iraqi2, you'll be reminded that not all Iraqis are the same. The more you discriminate among individuals covered by the same label, the less likely you are to discriminate against any group.

- Avoid polarization. Polarization, often referred to as the fallacy of "either/or," is the tendency to look at the world and to describe it in terms of extremes—good or bad, positive or negative, healthy or sick, brilliant or stupid, rich or poor, and so on. Polarized statements come in many forms; for example: After listening to the evidence, I'm still not clear who the good guys are and who the bad guys are. Well, are you for us or against us? College had better get me a good job. Otherwise, this has been a big waste of time.

Most people and events exist somewhere between the extremes of good and bad, healthy and sick, brilliant and stupid, rich and poor. Yet there seems to be a strong tendency to view only the extremes and to categorize people, objects, and events in terms of these polar opposites.

The & Box, Polarizing Terms, provides an experience illustrating the influence of language in polarization.

&

Polarizing Terms

The tendency to polarize can be easily demonstrated with a simple exercise. Try filling in the opposites for each of the following words:

		Opposite
tall	___:___:___:_X_:___:____:___	________
heavy	___:___:___:_X_:___:___:___	________
strong	___:___:___:_X_:____:___:___	________
happy	___:___:___:_X_:___:___:___	________
legal	___:___:___:_X_:___:___:____	________
high	___:___:___:_X_:___:____:___	________
big	___:___:___:_X_:___:___:___	________
sweet	___:___:___:_X_:____:___:___	________
nervous	___:___:___:_X_:___:___:___	________
bright	___:___:___:_X_:___:___:____	________

Filling in the opposites should have been relatively easy and quick. The words should also have been fairly short. Further, if various different people supplied the opposites, there would be a high degree of agreement among them. Now try to fill in the middle positions (the positions marked with an X) with words meaning, for example, "midway between tall and short," "midway between heavy and light," and so on. Do this before reading any farther.

These midway responses (compared to the opposites) were probably more difficult to think of and took you more time. The responses should also have been long words or phrases of several words. Further, different people would probably agree less on these midway responses than on the opposites.

This exercise illustrates the ease with which we can think and talk in opposites and the difficulty we have in thinking and talking about the middle. But recognize that the vast majority of cases exist between extremes. Don't allow the ready availability of extreme terms to obscure the reality of what lies in between.

In some cases, of course, it's legitimate to talk in terms of two values. For example, either this thing you're holding is a pencil or it isn't. Clearly, the classes "pencil" and "not-pencil" include all possibilities. There is no problem with this kind of statement. Similarly, you may say that a student either will pass this course or will not, as these two categories include all the possibilities. You create problems, however, when you use this either/or form in situations in which it's inappropriate; for example, "The supervisor is either for us or against us." The two choices simply don't include all possibilities: The supervisor may be for us in some things and against us in others, or he or she may be neutral. Right now there is a tendency to group people into pro- and antiwar, for example—and into similar pro- and anti- categories on abortion, taxes, same-sex marriage, and just about every important political or social issue. Similarly, you see examples of polarization in opinions about the Middle East, with some people entirely and totally supportive of one side and others entirely and totally supportive of the other side. But clearly these extremes do not include all possibilities and polarized thinking actually prevents us from considering the vast middle ground that exists on all such issues.

- **Avoid static evaluation.** Language changes very slowly, especially when compared to the rapid pace at which people and things change. When you retain an evaluation of a person, despite the inevitable changes in the person, you're engaging in static evaluation. Alfred Korzybski, the founder of General Semantics, used an interesting illustration in this connection: In a tank there is a large fish and many small fish that are its natural food source. Given freedom in the tank, the large fish will eat the small fish. After some time, the tank is partitioned, with the large fish on one side and the small fish on the other, divided only by glass. For a time, the large fish will try to eat the small fish but will fail; each time it tries, it will knock into the glass partition. After some time it will learn that trying to eat the small fish means difficulty, and it will no longer go after them. Now, however, the partition is removed, and the small fish swim all around the big fish. But the big fish does not eat them and in fact will die of starvation while its natural food swims all around. The large fish has learned a pattern of behavior, and even though the actual territory has changed, the map remains static.

  While you would probably agree that everything is in a constant state of flux, the relevant question is whether you act as if you know this. Do you act in accordance with the notion of change, instead of just accepting it intellectually? Do you treat your younger sister as if she were ten years old, or do you treat her like the twenty-year-old woman she has become? Your evaluations of yourself and others need to keep pace with the rapidly changing real world. Otherwise you'll be left with attitudes and beliefs—static evaluations—about a world that no longer exists.

  To guard against static evaluation, use an extensional device called the date: Mentally date your statements and especially your evaluations. Remember that Gerry

Smith$_{2010}$ is not Gerry Smith$_{2014}$; academic abilities$_{2010}$ are not academic abilities$_{2014}$.

Try It

Whenever you make a decision; form or change an attitude, belief, or opinion; or act one way or another review what you did against the six critical thinking strategies presented here. With practice the strategies should become a part of your thinking and behaving.

Strategies for

Criticizing

Criticism is often essential in helping someone learn a skill or correct some failing. Sometimes, it's asked for (*How do I look? Is this jacket ok for the interview?*) and sometimes it isn't. The critic is often himself or herself criticized for being critical. So anticipate this. Nevertheless, there are times when criticism is needed. Constructively expressed, criticism can serve useful purposes. Here are some strategies to make your criticism more successful.

- **Focus on the event or behavior rather than rather than on personality.** For example, say, "This paper has four typos and has to be redone" rather than "You're a lousy typist; do this over." In offering criticism, be specific. Instead of saying, "This paper is weak," say, "I think the introduction wasn't clear enough. Perhaps a more specific statement of purpose would have worked better."

- **Be positive.** Try to state criticism positively, if at all possible. Rather than saying, "You look terrible in black," it might be more helpful to say, "You look best in bright colors." In this way, you're also being constructive; you're explaining what can be done to make the situation better. If you do express criticism that seems to prove destructive, it may be helpful to offer a direct apology or to disclaim any harmful intentions. In your positive statement of criticism, try to demonstrate that your criticism stems from your caring and concern for the other person. Instead of saying, "The introduction to your report is boring," say, "I really want your report to be great; I'd open with some humor to get the group's attention." Or say, "I want you to make a good impression. I think the dark suit would work better."

- **Avoid threatening punishment.** Avoid implying that because of the criticism, approval or affection will be withdrawn. When you criticize specific behavior rather than the person as a whole, this is less likely to happen.

- **Own your thoughts and feelings.** Instead of saying, "Your report was unintelligible," say, "I had difficulty following your ideas." At the same time, avoid mind reading. Instead of saying, "Don't you care about the impression you make? This report is terrible," say, "I think I would use a stronger introduction and a friendlier writing style."

- **Be clear.** Many people tend to phrase their criticism ambiguously, thinking that this will hurt less. Research suggests, however, that although ambiguous criticism may appear more polite, it also will appear less honest, less competent, and not necessarily more positive.

- **Avoid ordering or directing.** Be careful that you don't attack a person's negative face needs by ordering or telling them what they should or should not do. Try identifying possible alternatives. Instead of saying, "Don't be so forward when you're first introduced to someone," consider saying, "I think people respond better to a less forward approach."

- **Consider the context of the criticism.** Generally, it's best to express criticism in situations where you can interact with the person and express your attitudes in dialogue rather than monologue. By this principle, then, your first choice would be to express criticism face-to-face and your second choice would be by telephone; a distant third choice would be by letter, memo, or e-mail. Also, try to express your criticism in private. This is especially important when you are dealing with members of cultures in which public criticism can result in a serious loss of face.

As a receiver of criticism, consider the motivation behind the criticism. Some criticism, perhaps most, is well intentioned and is designed to help you improve your performance or benefit you in some way. But some criticism is motivated by less noble purposes and may be designed to hurt or to humiliate you. Criticism that is not constructive needs to be examined mindfully. Criticism uttered in conflict or in times of rising emotions may be harsher and more hurtful than criticism given in calmer moments.

Try It

A good way to practice criticism is to formulate a criticism for some fictional character—perhaps an inept interview or an ineffective attempt to ask for a date in a television sitcom or on a YouTube video.

Strategies for

Dialogue

A dialogue is a two-way interaction. Each person is both speaker and listener, sender and receiver. In dialogic communication there is concern for the other person and for the relationship between the two people. The objective of dialogue is mutual understanding and empathy. There is respect for the other person, not because of what this person can do or give, but simply because this person is a human being and therefore deserves to be treated honestly and sincerely.

In a dialogic interaction, you respect the other person enough to allow that person the right to make his or her own choices without coercion, without the threat of punishment, without fear or social pressure. A dialogic communicator respects other people enough to believe that they can make their own decisions and implicitly or explicitly lets them know that whatever choices they make, they will still be respected as people.

In contrast, a monologue is communication in which one person speaks and the other listens; there's no real interaction among participants. The term *monologic communication* is an extension of this basic definition and refers to communication in which there is no genuine interaction, in which you speak without any real concern for the other person's feelings or attitudes. The monologic communicator is concerned only with his or her own goals and is interested in the other person only insofar as that person can be used to achieve those goals. In monologic interaction, you communicate what will advance your own goals, prove most persuasive, and benefit you.

Not surprisingly, effective communication is based not on monologue but on its opposite, dialogue. Here are some useful strategies for achieving dialogic communication:

- **Avoid negative criticism and negative personal judgments.** Practice using positive criticism ("I like those first two explanations best; they were really well reasoned") rather than negative criticism ("I didn't like that explanation") and negative personal judgments ("You're not a very good listener, are you?").

- **Keep the channels of communication open** ("I really don't know what I did that offended you, but tell me. I don't want to hurt you again"). At the same time, you avoid dysfunctional communication such as avoiding the topic or talking about irrelevancies.

- **Paraphrase or summarize what the other person has said.** This will help ensure accurate understanding. You rarely demonstrate through paraphrase or summary that you understand the other person's meaning.

- **Request clarification as necessary.** Ask for the other person's point of view because of a genuine interest in the other person's perspective; request clarification of the other person's perspectives or ideas.

- **Avoid requesting self-approval statements.** Avoid making positive statements about yourself or request statements of approval from others ("How did you like the way I told that guy off? Clever, no?").

Try It

Try the strategies for dialogue during your next conversation. Afterwards, reflect on your use of dialogue versus monologue. How well did you do? What could you have done better? How did the other person do? What would you have liked the other person to do that he or she didn't?

Strategies for

Disclaiming

Disclaimers are statements that aim to ensure that your messages will be understood as you wish it to be and will not reflect negatively on you. Often these are messages that others may react to negatively and disclaimers are designed to prevent or lessen this negative reaction. Disclaimers are messages that preface your main messages. Here are five types of disclaimers, each of which suggests a good strategy for getting your message received as you want.

- **Hedge.** Hedging helps you to separate yourself from the message so that if your listeners reject your message, they need not reject you (for example, "I may be wrong here, but . . ."). Hedging also enables you to cushion your being proven wrong. If, on the other hand, you were to say, "I know I'm right" (definitely not a disclaimer) and are then proven wrong, you're likely to feel some degree of discomfort or embarrassment.

- **Credential yourself.** Credentialing helps you establish your credibility, your believability. It helps you establish your special qualifications for saying what you're about to say ("Don't get me wrong, I'm not homophobic" or "As someone who telecommutes, I . . .").

- **Ask for a sin license.** Sin licenses are statements that ask listeners for permission to deviate in some way from some normally accepted convention, to violate the norms of discussion ("I know this may not be the place to discuss business, but . . .").

- **Establish your cognitive abilities.** Cognitive disclaimers help you make the case that you're in full possession of your faculties ("I know you'll think I'm drunk, but I'm perfectly sober" or "Don't think I'm exaggerating, I'm just reporting what I heard").

- **Appeal for the suspension of judgment.** Such appeals ask listeners to hear you out before making a judgment ("Don't hang up on me until you hear my side of the story"). These appeals are often used with excuses or apologies as in "I know you're angry but please hear me out."

Generally, disclaimers are effective when you think you might offend listeners in, say, telling a joke ("I don't usually like these types of jokes, but . . ."). In one study, for example, 11-year-old children were read a story about someone whose actions created negative effects. Some children heard the story with a disclaimer, and others heard the same story without a disclaimer. When the children were asked to indicate how the person should be punished, those who heard the story with a disclaimer recommended significantly lower punishments.

Disclaimers, however, can also get you into trouble. For example, to preface remarks with "I'm no liar" may well lead listeners to think that perhaps you are lying. Also, if you use too many disclaimers, you may be perceived as someone who doesn't have any strong convictions or as one who wants to avoid responsibility for just about everything. This seems especially true of hedges.

In responding to statements containing disclaimers, it's often necessary to respond to both the disclaimer and to the statement. By doing so, you let the speaker know that you heard the disclaimer and that you aren't going to view this communication negatively. Appropriate responses might be: "I know you're not sexist, but I don't agree that . . ." or "Well, perhaps we should discuss the money now even if it doesn't seem right."

Try It

Try first to identify disclaimers in the conversations of others. Then, when the need arises and you want to encourage your listeners' receptivity, try one of these strategies. Too many too often will naturally create problems.

Strategies for

Emotional Expression

Emotional expression is an inevitable part of communication in all its forms. But, it's often difficult, especially for men who have trouble expressing the softer emotions. Here are some strategies for making this often difficult part of communication more effective and more comfortable.

- **Be specific.** Consider, for example, the frequently heard "I feel bad." Does it mean "I feel guilty" (because I lied to my best friend)? "I feel lonely" (because I haven't had a date in the last two months)? "I feel depressed" (because I failed that last exam)? Specificity helps. Describe also the intensity with which you feel the emotion: "I feel so angry I'm thinking of quitting the job." "I feel so hurt I want to cry." Learn the vocabulary to describe your emotions and feelings in specific and concrete terms. See the & Box, Emotion Words, for a list of terms for describing your emotions verbally.

Emotion Words

The terms included for each basic emotion provide you with lots of choices for expressing the intensity level you're feeling. For example, if you're extremely fearful then *terror* or *dread* might be appropriate but if your fear is mild, then perhaps *apprehension* or *concern* might be an appropriate term. Also included are antonyms, providing additional choices for emotional expression.

- **Joy** happiness, bliss, cheer, contentment, delight, ecstasy, enchantment, enjoyment, felicity, rapture, gratification, pleasure, satisfaction, well-being. *Antonyms*: sadness, sorrow, unhappiness, woe, depression, gloom, misery, pain.
- **Trust** confidence, belief, hope, assurance, faith, reliance, certainty, credence, certitude, conviction. *Antonyms*: distrust, disbelief, mistrust, uncertainty.
- **Fear** anxiety, apprehension, awe, concern, consternation, dread, fright, misgiving, phobia, trepidation, worry, qualm, terror. *Antonyms*: courage, fearlessness, heroism, unconcern.
- **Surprise** amazement, astonishment, awe, eye-opener, incredulity, jolt, revelation, shock, unexpectedness, wonder, startle, catch off-guard, unforeseen. *Antonyms*: expectation, assurance, confidence, fear, intention, likelihood, possibility, prediction, surmise
- **Sadness** dejected, depressed, dismal, distressed, grief, loneliness, melancholy, misery, sorrowful, unhappiness. *Antonyms*: happiness, gladness, joy, cheer
- **Disgust** abhorrence, aversion, loathing, repugnance, repulsion, revulsion, sickness, nausea, offensiveness. *Antonyms*: admiration, desire, esteem, fondness, liking, loving, reverence, respect
- **Anger** acrimony, annoyance, bitterness, displeasure, exasperation, fury, ire, irritation, outrage, rage, resentment, tantrum, umbrage, wrath, hostility. *Antonyms*: calmness, contentment, enjoyment, peace, joy, pleasantness.
- **Anticipation** contemplation, prospect, expectancy, hope, foresight, expectation, foreboding, forecast, forethought. *Antonyms*: unreadiness, doubt, uncertainty.

- **Describe the reasons you're feeling as you are.** "I'm feeling guilty because I was unfaithful." "I feel lonely; I haven't had a date for the last two months." "I'm really depressed from failing that last exam." If your feelings were influenced by something the person you're talking to did or said, describe this also. For example, "I felt so angry when you said you wouldn't help me". "I felt hurt when you didn't invite me to the party."

- **Address mixed feelings.** Very often feelings are a mixture of several emotions, sometimes even of conflicting emotions. If you have such mixed feelings—and you really want the other person to understand you—then address these mixed or conflicting feelings. "I want so much to stay with Pat and yet I fear I'm losing my identity." Or, "I feel anger and hatred, but at the same time I feel guilty for what I did."

- **Anchor your emotions in the present.** Coupled with specific description and the identification of the reasons for your feelings, such statements might look like this: "I feel like a failure right now; I've erased this computer file three times today." "I felt foolish when I couldn't think of that formula." "I feel stupid when you point out my grammatical errors."

- **Own your feelings; take personal responsibility for your feelings.** Consider the following statements: "You make me angry." "You make me feel like a loser." "You make me feel stupid." "You make me feel like I don't belong here." In each of these statements, the speaker blames the other person for the way he or she is feeling. Of course, you know, on more sober reflection, that no one can make you feel anything. Others may do things or say things to you, but it is you who interpret them. That is, you develop feelings as a result of the interaction between what these people say, for example, and your own interpretations. Owning feelings means taking responsibility for them—acknowledging that your feelings are your feelings. The best way to own your statements is to use I-messages rather than the kinds of you-messages given above. With this acknowledgment of responsibility, the above statements would look like these: "I get angry when you come home late without calling." "I begin to think of myself as a loser when you criticize me in front of my friends." "I feel so stupid when you use medical terms that I don't understand." "When you ignore me in public, I feel like I don't belong here." These rephrased statements identify and describe your feelings about those behaviors; they don't attack the other person or demand that he or she change certain behaviors and consequently don't encourage defensiveness. With I-message statements, it's easier for the other person to acknowledge behaviors and to offer to change them. For good or ill, some social network sites (and the same is true with blogs) make it very easy to *not* own your own messages by enabling you to send comments anonymously.

- **Ask for what you want.** Depending on the emotions you're feeling, you may want the listener to assume a certain role or just listen or offer advice. Let the listener know what you want. Use I-messages to describe what, if anything, you want the listener to do: "I'm feeling sorry for myself right now; just give me some space. I'll give you a call in a few days." Or, more directly: "I'd prefer to be alone right now." Or, "I need advice." Or, "I just need someone to listen to me."

- **Respect emotional boundaries.** Each person has a different level of tolerance for communication about emotions or communication that's emotional. Be especially alert to nonverbal cues that signal that boundaries are near to being broken. And, it's often useful to simply ask, "Would you rather change the subject?"

Try It

Before trying these strategies in an actual communication situation, consider expressing emotions by yourself to perhaps a fictitious situation—try visualizing yourself expressing yourself to some character in a novel or drama. Then gradually apply the strategies noted here in real communication interactions.

Strategies for

Emotional Responding

Expressing your feelings is only half of the process of emotional communication; the other half is listening to and responding to the feelings of others. Here are a few strategies for making an often difficult process a little easier.

- **Look for cues to understand the individual's feelings.** For example, overly long pauses, frequent hesitations, eye contact avoidance, or excessive fidgeting may be a sign of discomfort that it might be wise to talk about. Similarly, look for inconsistent messages, as when someone says that "everything is okay" while expressing facial sadness; these are often clues to mixed feelings. But be sure to use any verbal or nonverbal cues as hypotheses, never as conclusions. Check your perceptions before acting on them. Treat inferences as inferences and not as facts.

- **Look for cues as to what the person wants you to do.** Sometimes, all the person wants is for someone to listen. Don't equate (as the stereotypical male supposedly does) "responding to another's feelings" with "solving the other person's problems." Instead, provide a supportive atmosphere that encourages the person to express his or her feelings.

- **Listen.** Listening closely and showing that you're listening will encourage the person to talk should he or she wish to. Paraphrase the speaker. Express understanding of the speaker's feelings. Ask questions as appropriate. For more on this see the *Active Listening* chapter.

- **Empathize.** See the situation from the point of view of the speaker. Don't evaluate the other person's feelings. For example, comments such as "Don't cry; it wasn't worth it" or "You'll get promoted next year" can easily be interpreted to mean "Your feelings are wrong or inappropriate."

- **Focus on the other person.** Interjecting your own similar past situations is often useful for showing your understanding, but it may create problems if it refocuses the conversation away from the other person. Show interest by encouraging the person to explore his or her feelings. Use simple encouragers like "I see" or "I understand." Or ask questions to let the speaker know that you're listening and that you're interested.

- **Remember the irreversibility of communication.** Whether expressing emotion or responding to the emotions of others, it's useful to recall the irreversibility of communication. You won't be able to take back an insensitive or disconfirming response. Responses to another's emotional expressions are likely to have considerable impact, so be especially mindful to avoid inappropriate responding.

Try It

Try out these strategies the next time someone unloads their feelings. It should make the experience a lot easier for both.

Strategies for

Empathy

Empathy is feeling what another person feels from that person's point of view without losing your own identity. Empathy enables you to understand emotionally what another person is experiencing. (To sympathize, in contrast, is to feel the person—to feel sorry or happy for the person, for example.) Women, research shows, are perceived as more empathic and engage in more empathic communication than do men. So following these suggestions may come more easily to women.

Empathy is best expressed in two distinct parts: thinking empathy and feeling empathy. In thinking empathy you express an understanding of what the other person means. For example, when you paraphrase someone's comment, showing that you understand the meaning the person is trying to communicate, you're communicating thinking empathy. The second part is feeling empathy; here you express your feeling of what the other person is feeling. You demonstrate a similarity between what you're feeling and what the other person is feeling. Often you'll respond with both thinking and feeling empathy in the same brief response; for example, when a friend tells you of problems at home, you may respond by saying, for example, "Your problems at home do seem to be getting worse. I can imagine why you feel so angry at times."

Here are a few more specific strategies to help you communicate both your feeling and your thinking empathy more effectively:

- **Be clear.** Make it clear that you're trying to understand, not to evaluate, judge, or criticize.

- **Focus**. Maintain eye contact, an attentive posture, and physical closeness to focus your concentration. Express involvement through facial expressions and gestures.

- **Reflect.** In order to check the accuracy of your perceptions and to show your commitment to understanding the speaker, reflect back to the speaker the feelings that you think are being expressed. Offer tentative statements about what you think the person is feeling; for example, "You seem really angry with your father" or "I hear some doubt in your voice."

- **Disclose.** When appropriate, use your own self-disclosures to communicate your understanding; but be careful that you don't refocus the discussion on yourself.

- **Address mixed messages.** At times you may want to identify and address any mixed messages that the person is sending as a way to foster more open and honest communication. For example, if your friend verbally expresses contentment but shows nonverbal signs of depression, it may be prudent to question the possible discrepancy.

- **Acknowledge importance.** Make it clear that you understand the depth of a person's feelings.

Try It

The next time you talk with someone—especially about their feelings—try to express both thinking and feeling empathy by being clear, focusing, reflecting, disclosing, addressing mixed messages, and acknowledging the importance of the other person's feelings.

Strategies for

Expressiveness

Expressiveness is the skill of communicating genuine involvement in the conversation; it entails, for example, taking responsibility for your thoughts and feelings, encouraging expressiveness or openness in others, and providing appropriate feedback. As you can easily appreciate, these are the qualities that make a conversation exciting and satisfying. Expressiveness includes both verbal and nonverbal messages and often involves revealing your emotions and your normally hidden self.
Here are a few strategies for communicating expressiveness.

- **Smile.** Your smile is probably your most expressive feature and it will likely be much appreciated.

Real and Fake Smiles

Nonverbal researchers distinguish two kinds of smiles: the real and the fake. The real smile, known as the Duchenne smile, is genuine; it's an unconscious movement that accurately reflects your feelings at the time. The fake smile, on the other hand, is conscious.

Distinguishing between these two is crucial in a wide variety of situations. For example, you distinguish between these smiles when you make judgments as to whether someone is genuinely pleased at your good fortune or really jealous. You distinguish between these smiles when you infer that the person really likes you or is just being polite. In each of these cases, you're making judgments as to whether or not someone is lying. Not surprisingly, then, Duchenne smiles are responded to positively and fake smiles—especially if they're obvious—are responded to negatively.

- **Use vocal variation.** Vary your vocal rate, pitch, volume, and rhythm to convey involvement and interest. Vary your language; avoid clichés and trite expressions, which signal a lack of originality and personal involvement.

- **Use appropriate gestures.** Give special attention to gestures that focus on the other person rather than yourself. Maintain eye contact and lean toward the person; at the same time, avoid self-touching gestures or directing your eyes to others in the room.

- **Give feedback.** Give both verbal and nonverbal feedback to show that you're listening. Such feedback promotes relationship satisfaction. For more on this see the *Feedback* chapter.

- **Communicate expressiveness in ways that are culturally sensitive.** Some cultures (Italian, for example) encourage expressiveness and teach children to be expressive. Other cultures (Japanese and Thai, for example) encourage a more reserved response style. Some cultures (Arab and many Asian cultures, for example) consider expressiveness by women in business settings to be inappropriate.

Try It

Think about the expressiveness of the people you know who are extremely popular and those who are significantly less popular. In what ways do these groups differ in expressiveness? How would you describe your own expressiveness?

Strategies for

Feedback

Feedback refers to messages that you receive in response to your own messages. You get these messages from yourself and from those with whom you're communicating. When you send a message—say, in speaking to another person—you also hear yourself. That is, you get feedback from your own messages; you hear what you say, you feel the way you move, you see what you write. In addition to this self-feedback, you also get feedback from others. This feedback can take many forms. A frown or a smile, a yea or a nay, a returned poke or a retweet, a pat on the back or a punch in the mouth are all types of feedback.

Feedback tells the speaker what effect he or she is having on listeners. On the basis of feedback, the speaker may adjust, modify, strengthen, deemphasize, or change the content or form of the messages. For example, if someone laughs at your joke (giving you positive feedback), it may encourage you to tell another one. If the feedback is negative—no laughing, just blank stares—then you may resist relaying another "humorous" story.

Take a look at the & Box, Feedback Choices, for an idea of the types of feedback you might communicate.

Feedback Choices

Each feedback opportunity presents you with choices along at least the following five dimensions: positive–negative, person focused–message focused, immediate–delayed, low monitored–high monitored, and supportive–critical. To use feedback effectively, you need to make educated choices along these dimensions.

- Positive–Negative. Feedback may be positive (you pay a compliment or pat someone on the back) or negative (you criticize someone or scowl). Positive feedback tells the speaker that he or she is on the right track and should continue communicating in essentially the same way. Negative feedback tells the speaker that something is wrong and that some adjustment should be made.

- Person Focused–Message Focused. Feedback may center on the person ("You're sweet" or "You have a great smile"). Or it may center on the message ("Can you repeat that number?" or "Your argument is a good one").

- Immediate–Delayed. In interpersonal situations, feedback is often sent immediately after the message is received; you smile or say something in response almost simultaneously with your receiving the message. In other communication situations, however, the feedback may be delayed. In interview situations, for example, the feedback may come weeks afterward. In media situations, some feedback comes immediately through Nielsen ratings, and other feedback comes much later through viewing and buying patterns.

- Low-Monitoring–High-Monitoring Feedback. This dimension refers to the degree to which feedback is a spontaneous and totally honest reaction (low-monitored feedback) or a carefully constructed, highly censored, response designed to serve a specific purpose (high-monitored feedback). In most communication situations, you probably give feedback spontaneously; at other times, however, you may be more guarded, as when your boss asks you how you like your job or when your grandparents ask what you think of your dinner.

- Supportive–Critical. Supportive feedback accepts the speaker and what the speaker says. It occurs, for example, when you console another, encourage him or her to talk, or otherwise confirm the person's definition of self. Critical feedback, on the other hand, is evaluative; it's judgmental. When you give critical feedback (whether positive or negative), you judge another's performance—as in, for example, coaching someone learning a new skill.

Realize that these categories are not exclusive. Feedback does not have to be either critical or supportive; it can be both. For example, in talking with someone who is trying to become a more effective interviewer, you might critically evaluate a practice interview but also express support for the effort.

Here are a few strategies for giving effective feedback:

- **Focus on the behavior or the message.** Avoid focusing on the motives behind the message or behavior. Say, for example, "You forgot my birthday" rather than "You don't love me."

- **Begin with the positive.** If your feedback is largely negative, try to begin with something positive. There are always positives if you look hard enough. The negatives will be much easier to take, after hearing some positives.

- **Ask for feedback on your feedback.** For example, a simple "Does this make sense?" or "Do you understand what I want our relationship to be?"

- **Give feedback calmly.** Avoid giving feedback (especially negative feedback) when you're angry and especially when your anger is likely to influence what you say.

The other half of the feedback equation is the person receiving the feedback. When you are the recipient of feedback, be sure to show your interest in feedback. This is vital information that will help you improve whatever you're doing. Encourage the feedback giver. Be open to hearing this feedback. Don't argue; don't be defensive.

Perhaps most important, check your perceptions. Do you understand the feedback? If not, ask questions. Not all feedback is easy to understand; after all, a wink, a backward head nod, or a smile can each signal a variety of different messages. When you don't understand the meaning of the feedback, ask for clarification (nondefensively, of course). Paraphrase the feedback you've just received to make sure you both understand it: "You'd be comfortable taking over the added responsibilities if I went back to school?"

Try It

Examine your customary way of giving people feedback. How does it compare to the strategies identified here? If they differ, try using one or two of these strategies the next time you're in the position where you have to give feedback.

Feedforward

Feedforward is information you provide before sending your primary messages; it reveals something about the messages to come and includes, for example, the preface or table of contents of a book, the opening paragraph of a chapter, movie previews, magazine covers, and introductions in public speeches.

Feedforward may be verbal ("Wait until you hear this one") or nonverbal (a prolonged pause or hands motioning for silence to signal that an important message is about to be spoken). Or, as is most often the case, it is some combination of verbal and nonverbal. For the functions of feedforward see the & Box, Feedforward Functions.

Feedforward Functions

Feedforward can serve at least these four functions.

- **To open the channels of communication.** Feedforward may communicate that the normal, expected, and accepted rules of interaction will be in effect. It tells you another person is willing to communicate. It's the "How are you?" and "Nice weather" greetings that are designed to maintain rapport and friendly relationships.

- **To preview the message.** Feedforward messages may, for example, preview the content ("I'm afraid I have bad news for you"), the importance ("Listen to this before you make a move"), the form or style ("I'll tell you all the gory details"), and the positive or negative quality of subsequent messages ("You're not going to like this, but here's what I heard"). The subject heading on your e-mail well illustrates this function of feedforward, as do the phone numbers and names that come up on your caller ID.
- **To disclaim.** The disclaimer (for more on this see the *Disclaiming* chapter) is a statement that aims to ensure that your message will be understood as you want it to be and that it will not reflect negatively on you. For example, you might use a disclaimer when you think that what you're going to say may be met with opposition. Thus, you might say in feedforward: "I'm not against immigration, but . . ." or "Don't think I'm homophobic, but . . ."
- **To Altercast.** Feedforward is often used to place the receiver in a specific role and to request responses in terms of this assumed role, a process called altercasting. For example, you might altercast by asking a friend, "As a future advertising executive, what do you think of corrective advertising?" This question casts your friend in the role of advertising executive (rather than parent, Democrat, or Baptist, for example) and asks that she or he answer from a particular perspective.

Here are a few strategies for giving effective feedforward:

- **Use feedforward to estimate the receptivity of the person to what you're going to say.** For example, before asking for a date, you'd probably want to use feedforward to test the waters and to see if you're likely to get a "yes" response. You might ask if the other person enjoys going out to dinner or if he or she is dating anyone seriously. Before asking a friend for a loan, you'd probably feedforward your needy condition and say something like, "I'm really strapped for cash and need to get my hands on $200 to pay my car loan" and wait for the other person to say (you hope), "Can I help?"

- **Use feedforward that's consistent with your subsequent message.** If your main message is one of bad news, then your feedforward needs to be serious and to help to prepare the other person for this bad news. You might, for example, say something like, "I need to tell you something you're not going to want to hear. Let's sit down."
- **The more important or complex the message, the more important and more extensive your feedforward needs to be.** For example, in public speaking, in which the message is relatively long, the speaker is advised to give fairly extensive feedforward or what is called an orientation or preview. At the start of a business meeting, the leader may give feedforward in the form of an agenda or meeting schedule.
- **Use feedforward to cushion shocking messages.** Omitting feedforward before a truly shocking message (for example, the terminal illness of a friend or relative) can make you seem insensitive or uncaring.

Try It

Observe the feedforward around you—in face-to-face interactions, in emails, in television sitcoms, in news broadcasts, and in just anywhere communication takes place. Identify the purposes they serve and analyze their effectiveness. How could these feedforwards have been made more effective?

Strategies for

Flexibility

Flexibility is a quality of thinking and behaving which enables you to vary your messages based on the unique situation in which you find yourself. One measure of flexibility asks you to consider how true you believe certain statements are—— statements such as

- "People should be frank and spontaneous in conversation" or
- "When angry, a person should say nothing rather than say something he or she will be sorry for later."

The "preferred" answer to all such questions is "sometimes true," underscoring the importance of flexibility in all communication situations.

As you can appreciate, flexibility is especially important when communicating your feelings, be they positive or negative. It's especially important in emotional communication because it's in times of emotional arousal that you're likely to forget the varied choices for communicating that you have available. And of course this is exactly the time when you need to consider your choices. The greater your flexibility, the more likely you'll be to see the varied choices you do have for communicating in any situation.

Here are a few strategies to cultivate flexibility.

- **Consider your choices.** In every communication situation you have choices concerning whether or not you say anything, when you say something, to whom you say it, how you say it, through what channel you say it, and so on.

- **Focus on differences.** Realize that no two situations or people are exactly alike; consider what is different about this situation or person and take these differences into consideration as you analyze your choices and construct your messages.

- **Contextualize.** Recognize that communication always takes place in a context; discover what that unique context is and ask yourself how it might influence your messages. Communicating bad news during a joyous celebration, for example, needs to be handled quite differently from communicating good news.

- **Recognize constant change.** Become aware of the constant change in people and in things. Everything is in a state of flux. Even if the way you communicated last month was effective, that doesn't mean it will be effective today or tomorrow. Realize too that sudden changes (the death of a lover or a serious illness) will influence what are and what are not appropriate messages.

- **Appreciate your options.** Remind yourself of the fact that every situation offers you different options for communicating. Consider these options and try to predict the effects each option might have.

Try It

During your next conversation try some of the flexibility strategies by consciously asking yourself questions—how does this situation differ from other situations and in what way might appropriate responses differ? How is the context influencing the situation and in what way might I respond differently? How have things/people changed and what does this mean to my communication behavior? And most important analyze your options—there is rarely (if ever) only one way to communicate. For any important interaction, you should be able to come up with at least three or four ways to communicate.

Another way to practice flexibility is to respond to a relationship question—such as that posed in Dear Abby-type columns—and generate as many possible answers as you can. You'll soon develop the habit of analyzing questions from varied points of view and will increase your flexibility quotient.

Strategies for

Flirting

Flirting is something everyone enjoys doing. If done well, it can result in the start of a wonderful relationship. But, if poorly done it can result in hostility. Here are a few nonverbal and verbal ways people flirt and some cautions to observe. The most general caution which applies to all the strategies is to recognize that different cultures view flirting very differently and to observe the prevailing cultural norms.

Here are a few strategies for flirting effectively and a few cautions to observe.

- **Maintain an open posture**; face the person; lean forward; tilt your head to one side (to get a clearer view of the person you're interested in). But, don't move so close that you make it uncomfortable for the other person.

- **Make eye contact** and maintain it for a somewhat longer than normal time; raise your eyebrows to signal interest; blink and move your eyes more than usual; wink. Be careful that your direct eye contact doesn't come off as leering or too invasive and avoid too much blinking—people will think you have something wrong with your eyes.

- **Smile** and otherwise display positive emotions with your facial expressions. Avoid overdoing this; laughing too loud at lame jokes is probably going to appear phony.

- **Touch the person's hand**. Be careful that the touching is appropriate and not perceived as intrusive.

- **Mirror the other's behaviors**. Don't overdo it. It will appear as if you're mimicking.
- **Introduce yourself**. By introducing yourself, you project an open and forthright personality. Avoid overly long or overly cute introductions.
- **Ask a question** (most commonly, Is this seat taken?). Avoid sarcasm or joking; these are likely to be misunderstood.
- **Compliment** ("great jacket"). Avoid any compliment that might appear too intimate or sexually suggestive.
- **Be polite**; respect the individuals positive and negative face needs. But, don't be overly polite; it will appear phony.

Try It

Try one or two or three of these strategies the next time you find yourself in a flirtatious mood. Just be careful not to overdo anything. For example, too many compliments will make you appear phony; so, compliment in moderation. Make progress in very small steps.

Strategies for

Friendship Development

Friendships exist because they serve important needs. On the basis of your experiences or your predictions, you select as friends those who will help to satisfy a variety of basic needs. Selecting friends on the basis of need satisfaction is similar to choosing a marriage partner, an employee, or any person who may be in a position to satisfy your needs. From these needs we can derive strategies for developing and maintaining these relationships.

Friendship Types

Not all friendships are the same; three types are especially important:

- The **friendship of reciprocity** is the ideal type, characterized by loyalty, self-sacrifice, mutual affection, and generosity. A friendship of reciprocity is based on equality: Each individual shares equally in giving and receiving the benefits and rewards of the relationship.

- In the **friendship of receptivity**, in contrast, there is an imbalance in giving and receiving; one person is the primary giver and one the primary receiver. This is a positive imbalance, however, because each person gains something from the relationship. The different needs of both the person who receives and the person who gives affection are satisfied. This is the friendship that may develop between a teacher and a student or between a doctor and a patient. In fact, a difference in status is essential for the friendship of receptivity to develop.
- The **friendship of association** is a transitory one. It might be described as a friendly relationship rather than a true friendship. Associative friendships are the kind we often have with classmates, neighbors, or coworkers. There is no great loyalty, no great trust, no great giving or receiving. The association is cordial but not intense.

- **Serve a utility function.** Share your special talents, skills, or resources that will prove useful to your friend. If you're especially bright who might assist your friend in getting a better job or in introducing him or her to a possible romantic partner.

- **Engage in affirmation.** Affirm your friend's personal value and help your friend to recognize his or her best attributes, for example, communicates appreciation for your friend's leadership abilities, athletic prowess, or sense of humor.

- **Be ego supportive.** Be encouraging and helpful as the need arises.

- **Be stimulating.** Introduce your friend to new ideas and new ways of seeing the world.

- **Provide security.** Be protective, especially of the person's ego. Avoid calling attention to any weaknesses; be supportive and nonjudgmental.

Try It

Observing these functions in the media is probably the best way to begin examining friendship. For example, what friendship needs do the characters on *The Big Bang Theory* or *How I Met Your Mother* serve? Then, naturally, identify these same functions in your real life friendships and look for ways in which you can increase the extent to which you serve these functions and, at the same time, find friends who can help you with your needs.

Strategies for

Grief-Stricken Communication

Communicating with people who are experiencing grief, a common but difficult type of communication interaction, requires special care. A person may experience grief because of illness or death, the loss of a job or highly valued relationship (such as a friendship or romantic breakup), the loss of certain physical or mental abilities, the loss of material possessions (a house fire or stock losses), or the loss of some ability (for example, the loss of the ability to have children or to play the piano). For more on this type of communication see the *Emotional Expression* and *Emotional Responding* chapters. Each situation seems to call for a somewhat different set of dos and don'ts. Yet, there seem some general strategies as well.

The Five Stages of Grief

Elisabeth Kubler-Ross identified five stages of grief which seem accepted as the path many (but not all) people go through, whether the grief is occasioned by the death of a loved one, the loss of some physical function, or the loss of a home or relationship.

- **Denial**. You deny what has happened; you can't believe it.
- **Anger**. You become angry because of what happened.

- **Bargaining**. Often you bargain with God; *I'll change my way of life if you'll only spare his life.* Or, you might bargain with your relationship partner, *Will you come back if I stopped drinking?*
- **Depression**. The grief deepens and you realize the great loss you suffered. Your depression is normal.
- **Acceptance**. You accept the reality. Things will never return to "normal" but you accept the situation for what it is and are ready to move on.

- **Confirm the other person and the person's emotions.** A simple "You must be worried about finding another position" or "You must be feeling very alone right now" confirms the person's feelings. This type of expressive support lessens feelings of grief.

- **Give the person permission to grieve.** Let the person know that it's acceptable and okay with you if he or she grieves in the ways that feel most comfortable—for example, crying or talking about old times. Don't try to change the subject or interject too often. As long as the person is talking and seems to be feeling better for it, be supportive.

- **Avoid trying to focus on the bright side.** Avoid expressions such as "You're lucky you have some vision left" or "It's better this way; Pat was suffering so much." These expressions may easily be seen as telling people that their feelings should be redirected, that they should be feeling something different.

- **Encourage the person to express feelings and talk about the loss.** Most people will welcome this opportunity. On the other hand, don't try to force people to talk about experiences or feelings they may not be willing to share.

- **Be especially sensitive to leave-taking cues.** Behaviors such as fidgeting or looking at a clock, and statements such as "It's getting late" or "We can discuss this later," are hints that the other person is ready to end the conversation. Don't overstay your welcome.

- **Let the person know you care and are available.** Saying you're sorry is a simple but effective way to let the person know you care. Express your empathy; let the grief-stricken person know that you can feel (to some extent) what he or she is going through. But don't assume that your feelings, however empathic you are, are the same in depth or in kind. At the same time, let the person know that you are available—"If you ever want to talk, I'm here" or "If there's anything I can do, please let me know."

Try It

The next time you're talking with someone who is experiencing grief, try some of these strategies. But, realize that each situation is unique and so even when you follow the strategies and do everything according to the book, you may find that your comments are not appreciated or are not at all effective in helping the person feel any better. Use these cues to help you readjust your messages.

Strategies for avoiding

Heterosexist Talk

Unlike sexist language which seems to be fading, heterosexist or homophobic language is still very much with us and it will prove useful to identify some of the ways we can avoid talk that puts down gay men and lesbians. Heterosexist talk (and perhaps *homophobic talk* would be a more apt description) includes derogatory terms used for lesbians and gay men. For example, one study of the military showed that 80 percent of those surveyed heard offensive speech about gay men and lesbians and that 85 percent believed that such derogatory speech was "tolerated". You also see heterosexism in more subtle forms of language usage; for example, when you qualify a professional—as in "gay athlete" or "lesbian doctor"—and, in effect, say that athletes and doctors are not normally gay or lesbian.

Take a look at the & Box, Individual and Institutional Heterosexism, for a useful way of looking at this communication issue.

Individual and Institutional Heterosexism

Heterosexism exists on both an individual and an institutional level.

- **Individual heterosexism** consists of attitudes, behaviors, and language that disparage gay men and lesbians and includes the belief that all sexual behavior that is not heterosexual is unnatural and deserving of criticism and condemnation. These beliefs are at the heart of antigay violence and gay bashing. Individual heterosexism also includes such beliefs as the notions that homosexuals are more likely to commit crimes than are heterosexuals (there's actually no difference) and to molest children than are heterosexuals (actually, child molesters are overwhelmingly heterosexual, married men). It also includes the belief that homosexuals cannot maintain stable relationships or effectively raise children, beliefs that contradict research evidence.

- **Institutional heterosexism** is easy to identify. For example, the ban on gay marriage in most states and the fact that at this time only a handful of states allows gay marriage is a good example of institutional heterosexism. Other examples include the religions that bar gay men and lesbians from becoming priests, ministers, and rabbis, for example, and the many laws prohibiting adoption of children by gay people. In some cultures homosexual relations are illegal (for example, Pakistan, Yemen, and Iran, with sentences that can range from years in prison to death). And, interestingly enough, in some cultures homosexual relationships are illegal for men but legal for women (for example, in Palau, Cook Islands, Tonga, and Guyana).

- **Avoid offensive mannerisms.** Avoid using offensive nonverbal mannerisms that parody stereotypes when talking about gay men and lesbians. For example, do you respond to gay couples with the "startled eye blink"?

- **Avoid "complimenting" gay men and lesbians by saying that they "don't look it".** To gay men and lesbians, this is not a compliment. Similarly, expressing disappointment that a person is gay—often thought to be a compliment, as in comments such as "What a waste!"—is not really a compliment.

- **Avoid making the assumption that every gay or lesbian knows what every other gay or lesbian is thinking.** It's similar to asking a Japanese person why Sony is investing heavily in the United States.

- **Avoid the presumption of heterosexuality.** Usually, people assume the person they're talking to or about is heterosexual. And usually they're correct, because most people are heterosexual. At the same time, however, this presumption denies the lesbian or gay identity a certain legitimacy. The practice is very similar to the presumptions of whiteness and maleness that we have made significant inroads in eliminating.

- **Avoid relying on stereotypes.** Saying things like "Lesbians are so loyal" or "Gay men are so open with their feelings," ignore the reality of wide differences within any group and are potentially insulting to all groups.

- **Avoid overattribution.** This is the tendency to attribute just about everything a person does, says, and believes to the fact that the person is gay or lesbian? Every person (heterosexual and homosexual) is motivated by a variety of factors. Affectional orientation is just one of them.

- **Remember that relationship milestones are important to all people.** Ignoring anniversaries or birthdays of, say, a relative's partner is resented by everyone.

- **Use appropriate cultural identifiers**. *Gay* is the preferred term to refer to a man who has an affectional orientation toward other men, and *lesbian* is the preferred term for a woman who has an affectional orientation toward other women. ["Lesbian" means "homosexual woman," so the term *lesbian woman* is redundant.] *Homosexual* refers to both gay men and lesbians, and describes a same-sex sexual orientation. The definitions of *gay* and *lesbian* go beyond sexual orientation and refer to a self identification as a gay man or lesbian. *Gay* as a noun, although widely used, may be offensive in some contexts, as in "We have two gays on the team." Because most scientific thinking holds that sexuality is not a matter of choice, the terms *sexual orientation* and *affectional orientation* are preferred to *sexual preference* or *sexual status* (which is also vague). In the case of same-sex marriages—there are two husbands or two wives. In a male-male marriage, each person is referred to as *husband* and in the case of female-female marriage, each person is referred to as *wife*. Some same-sex couples—especially those who are not married—prefer the term "partner" or "lover". Whether married or not, your uncle's gay partner is also your uncle in the same way that your heterosexual aunt's husband is your uncle. Your sister's lover is your sister-in-law (though in many cases, the "in-law" is not technically accurate, it is the more culturally sensitive form to use) in the same way that your heterosexual brother's wife is your sister-in-law.

Try It

Examine your own language for traces of heterosexism. As you do, realize that heterosexist language will not only create barriers to communication but also that its absence will foster more meaningful communication: greater comfort, an increased willingness to disclose personal information, and a greater willingness to engage in future interactions.

Strategies for

Immediacy

Immediacy is the creation of closeness, a sense of togetherness, of oneness, between speaker and listener. When you communicate immediacy you convey a sense of interest and attention, a liking for and an attraction to the other person. Here are a few strategies for communicating immediacy (see the & box, Immediacy Payoffs, for some of its benefits) verbally and nonverbally.

Immediacy Payoffs

Immediacy has important payoffs. Immediacy behaviors will generally increase your perceived attractiveness and so in your relationship world, immediacy behaviors will generally prove helpful. In addition there is considerable evidence to show that immediacy behaviors are also effective in workplace communication, especially between supervisors and subordinates. For example, when a supervisor uses immediacy behaviors, he or she is seen by subordinates as interested and concerned; subordinates are therefore likely to communicate more freely and honestly about issues that can benefit the supervisor and the organization. Also, workers with supervisors who communicate immediacy behaviors have higher job satisfaction and motivation.

Immediacy behaviors of teachers, for example, have been found to contribute to the student having more positive feelings about the class, learning more, and evaluating their instructor more highly.

- **Self-disclose.** Reveal something significant about yourself. For more on this see the *Self-Disclosing* chapter.

- **Refer to the other person's good qualities.** Recall their dependability, intelligence, or character——"you're always so reliable."

- **Express a positive view.** Communicate, in word and expression, your positive view of the other person and of your relationship——"I'm sure glad you're my roommate; you know everyone."

- **Talk about commonalities.** Focusing on similarities is generally perceived positively so talk about things you and the other person have done together or share.

- **Demonstrate responsiveness.** Give feedback cues that indicate you want to listen more and that you're interested——"And what else happened?"

- **Express psychological closeness and openness.** Maintain physical closeness and arrange your body to exclude third parties.

- **Maintain appropriate eye contact.** Your eye contact should show interest and concern. Limit looking around at others.

- **Smile.** The smile is a universal sign of positiveness. Use it to express your interest in the other person.

- **Focus on the other person's remarks.** Make the speaker know that you heard and understood what was said, and give the speaker appropriate verbal and nonverbal feedback.

- **Express positiveness through your facial expressions.** It will help here if you think positively; often facial expressions—without your awareness—will communicate your "real" feelings. So, if you think negative thoughts and try to express positively facially, you're likely to give inconsistent signals, almost always perceived negatively.

- **Express immediacy with an awareness of personality differences.** Immediacy generates increased communication which not everyone wants. For example, your smile may encourage your colleague to come into your office to chat when all you wanted to do was be friendly but left alone. Also, recognize that because immediacy behaviors prolong and encourage in-depth communication, they may not be responded to favorably by persons who are fearful about communication and/or who want to get the interaction over with as soon as possible.

- **Express immediacy with cultural sensitivity.** Not all cultures or all people respond in the same way to immediacy messages. For example, in the United States immediacy behaviors are generally seen as friendly and appropriate. In other cultures, however, the same immediacy behaviors may be viewed as overly familiar——as presuming that a relationship is close when only acquaintanceship exists.

- **Secure feedback on your immediacy efforts.** Immediacy behaviors are ambiguous and can lead to false perceptions.

For example, you may find yourself in trouble when you intend your smile as friendly, as a way of saying "hello" but your colleague interprets it as flirting.

At the same time that you'll want to demonstrate these immediacy messages, try also to avoid non-immediacy messages such as speaking in a monotone, looking away from the person you're talking to, frowning while talking, rolling your eyes in disbelief, having a tense body posture, or avoiding gestures.

Try It

Try expressing immediacy by using just two or three or four of the above strategies. Then, at a later time, analyze your immediacy attempts and assess the possible effects. What can you do to increase the effectiveness of your immediacy behaviors?

Strategies for

Introductions

One of the communication situations that often creates difficulties is the introduction of one person to another person. Let's say you're with Jack and bump into Jill who stops to talk. Because they don't know each other, it's your job to introduce them. Generally, it's best to do this simply but with enough detail to provide a context for further interaction. It might go something like this: *Jill Williams, this is Jack Smith, who works with me at ABC as marketing manager. I went to college with Jill and, if I'm not mistaken, she has just returned from Hawaii.*

With this introduction Jack and Jill can say something to each other based on the information provided in this brief (32-word) introduction. They can talk about working at ABC, what it's like being a marketing manager, what Jill majored in, what Hawaii is like, what Jill did in Hawaii, and on and on. If you simply said: "Jack this is Jill; Jill, Jack" there would be virtually nothing for Jack and Jill to talk about.

Some introductions require special strategies, for example:

- **Admit it when you forget the person's name.** If you forget the person's name, the best thing to do here is to admit it and say something like: "I don't know why I keep thinking your name is Joe; I know it's not. I'm blocking." You're not the only one who forgets names, and few people take great offense when this happens.

- **Don't be forced to self-disclose.** If you don't want to reveal what your relationship with the person you're with is, don't.

Simple say, "This is Jack." You don't have to identify what your relationship to Jack is if you don't want to. And, hopefully, the other person won't ask. Of course, if you want to reveal your relationship, then do so. This is Jack, my lover, boyfriend, life partner, parole officer, or whatever term you want to use to define your relationship.

- **Be culturally sensitive.** In using names, it's best to be consistent with the norms operating in your specific culture. So, if just first names are exchanged in the introduction, use just first names. If the norm is to use first and last names, follow that pattern. Also, be consistent with the two people you introduce. Use just the first name for both or first name plus last name for both.

- **Observe rank and gender differences.** If the two people are of obviously different ranks, then the person of lower rank is introduced to the person of higher rank. Thus, you'd introduce the child to the adult, the junior executive to the senior executive, the student to the professor. Another commonly practiced rule is to introduce the man to the woman: *Marie, this is Stephen.* Or *Marie, I'd like to introduce Stephen to you.*

In the United States, the handshake is the most essential gesture of introduction. Take a look at the & Box, 6 Steps to Shaking Hands.

6 Steps to Shaking Hands

Here are six steps to an effective handshake in the United States. In other cultures, the firmness of the shake and the time the hand shake lasts, for example, will be different.

- **Make eye contact.** This is especially important at the beginning but maintain it throughout the handshake. Avoid looking away from the person or down at the floor or at your shaking hand.
- **Be positive.** Smile and otherwise signal positiveness. Avoid appearing static or negative.
- **Extend your entire right hand.** Don't extend just your fingers or your left hand.
- **Grasp firmly.** Grasp the other person's hand firmly but without so much pressure that it would be uncomfortable. Avoid grasping the other person's fingers as if you really don't want to shake hands but you're making a gesture to be polite.
- **Pump three times.** A handshake in the United States lasts about three to four seconds. In other cultures, it might be shorter or, more often, longer. Be careful that you don't give the person a "dead fish." Be careful that the other person's pumping doesn't lead you to withdraw your own pumping. Avoiding pumping much more than three times.
- **Release grasp while still maintaining eye contact.** Avoid holding the grasp for an overly long time or releasing it too early.

In Muslim cultures people hug same-sex people but not opposite-sex people. In Latin America, South America, and the Mediterranean, people are more likely to hug (and perhaps kiss on the cheek) than are Northern Europeans, Asians, and many from the United States. Asians are more likely to bow, with lower bows required when someone of lower status meets someone of higher status, for example, an intern meeting a company executive or a private meeting a general.

Try It

One great way to learn about introductions is to observe them in movies and television dramas and sitcom. Here you'll see both effective and ineffective introductions. What distinguishes effective from ineffective introductions?

Strategies for

Listening

Listening is actually a complex of processes and skills and so it's convenient to divide the listening process into stages or steps. These stages seem to get at most, if not all, of the essential listening processes and, more important, enables you to identify the relevant strategies at each stage.

Listening at the Receiving Stage. The first stage in the process of listening is receiving the message. At this stage you listen not only to what is said (verbally and nonverbally) but also to what is omitted. You receive, for example, your boss's summary of your accomplishments as well as the omission of your shortcomings or, perhaps, vice versa. Effective reception, then, consists of receiving what is as well as what is not said. Here are just three strategies for improving your listening reception:

- **Focus your attention on the speaker's verbal and nonverbal messages, on what is said and on what isn't said.** Avoid focusing your attention on what you'll say next; if you begin to rehearse your responses, you're going to miss what the speaker says next.
- **Avoid distractions in the environment.** If necessary, shut off the stereo or and turn off your phone. Put down the newspaper or magazine; close your laptop.
- **Maintain your role as listener and avoid interrupting.** Avoid interrupting as much as possible. It will only prevent you from hearing what the speaker is saying.

Listening at the Understanding Stage. The second stage of listening is understanding the message. That is, after receiving the message, you process it; you extract the meaning from the message. You can improve your listening understanding with several strategies:

- **Avoid assuming you understand what the speaker is going to say before he or she actually says it.** If you do make assumptions, these will likely prevent you from accurately listening to what the speaker wants to say.
- **See the speaker's messages from the speaker's point of view.** Avoid judging the message until you fully understand it as the speaker intended it.
- **Ask questions for clarification.** If necessary; ask for additional details or examples if they're needed. This shows not only that you're listening—which the speaker will generally appreciate—but also that you want to learn more. Material that is not clearly understood is likely to be easily forgotten.
- **Rephrase (paraphrase) the speaker's ideas into your own words.** This can be done silently or aloud. If done silently, it will help you rehearse and learn the material; if done aloud, it also helps you confirm your understanding of what the speaker is saying and gives the speaker an opportunity to clarify any misunderstandings.

Listening at the Remembering Stage. The third stage of listening is remembering the message. It would help little if you received and understood the message but didn't remember it. If you want to remember what someone says or the names of various people, this information needs to pass from your short-term memory (the memory you use, say, to remember a phone number just long enough to write it down) into long-term memory (or relatively permanent memory). Short-term memory is limited in capacity—you can hold only a small amount of information there. Long-term memory is unlimited. To facilitate the passage of information from short- to long-term memory, here are FOUR strategies (Focus, Organize, Unite, and Repeat):

- **Focus your attention on the central ideas.** Even in the most casual of conversations, there are central ideas. Fix these in your mind. Repeat these ideas to yourself as you continue to listen. Avoid focusing on minor details that often lead to detours in listening and in conversation.
- **Organize what you hear.** Summarize the message in a more easily retained form, but take care not to ignore crucial details or qualifications. If you chunk the material into categories, you'll be able to remember more information. For example, if you want to remember 15 or 20 items to buy in the supermarket, you'll remember more of them if you group them into chunks—say, produce, canned goods, and meats.
- **Unite the new with the old.** Relate new information to what you already know. Avoid treating new information as totally apart from all else you know. There's probably some relationship and if you identify it, you're more like to remember the new material.
- **Repeat names and key concepts to yourself or, if appropriate, aloud.** By repeating the names or key concepts, you in effect rehearse these names and concepts, and as a result you'll find them easier to learn and remember. If you're introduced to Alice, you'll stand a better chance of remembering her name if you say, "Hi, Alice" than if you say just "Hi."

Reasoning Fallacies

When listening to logical or seemingly logical arguments, listen for what are called the *fallacies of reasoning*: arguments that appear to address issues but really don't. Here are 10 such fallacies. Learn to spot fallacies in the conversations of others, and be sure to avoid them in your own.

- **Anecdotal evidence.** Often you'll hear people use anecdotal evidence to "prove" a point: "Women are like that; I know, because I have three sisters." "That's the way Japanese managers are; I've seen plenty of them." One reason this type of "evidence" is inadequate is that it relies on too few observations; it's usually a clear case of over-generalizing on the basis of too few instances. A second reason anecdotal evidence is inadequate is that one person's observations may be unduly clouded by his or her own attitudes and beliefs; your personal attitudes toward women or Japanese-style management, for example, may influence your perception of their behaviors.
- **Straw man.** A straw man argument (like a man made of straw) is a contention that's easy to knock down. In this fallacy a speaker creates an easy-to-destroy simplification of an opposing position (that is, a straw man) and then proceeds to smash it. But, of course, if the opposing case were presented fairly and without bias, it wouldn't be so easy to demolish.

- **Appeal to tradition.** Often used as an argument against change, the appeal to tradition claims that some proposed innovation is wrong or should not be adopted because it was never done before. This fallacious argument is used repeatedly by those who don't want change. But, of course, the fact that something has not been done before says nothing about its value or whether or not it should be done now.
- **Bandwagon.** In the bandwagon fallacy, often referred to as an argument ad populum (to the people), the speaker tries to persuade the audience to accept or reject an idea or proposal because "everybody's doing it" or because the "right" people are doing it. The speaker urges you to jump on this large and popular bandwagon—or be left out by yourself. This is a popular technique in political elections; campaigns trumpet the results of polls in an effort to get undecided voters to jump on the bandwagon of the leading candidate. After all, you don't want to vote for a loser. When this technique is used ethically--when it's true--it's referred to a social proof.
- **Testimonial.** The testimonial technique involves using the image associated with some person to secure your approval (if you respect the person) or your rejection (if you don't respect the person). This is the technique of advertisers who use actors dressed up to look like doctors or plumbers or chefs to sell their products. Sometimes this technique takes the form of using only vague and general "authorities," as in "experts agree," "scientists say," "good cooks know," or "dentists advise."

- **Transfer.** In transfer the speaker associates her or his idea with something you respect (to gain your approval) or with something you detest (to gain your rejection). For example, a speaker might portray a proposal for condom distribution in schools as a means for "saving our children from AIDS" (to encourage acceptance) or as a means for "promoting sexual promiscuity" (to encourage disapproval). Sports-car manufacturers try to get you to buy their cars by associating them with high status and sex appeal; promoters of exercise clubs and diet plans attempt to associate them with health, self-confidence, and interpersonal appeal.
- **Plain folks.** Using the plain folks device, the speaker identifies himself or herself with the audience. The speaker is good—the "reasoning" goes—because he or she is one of the people, just plain folks like everyone else. Of course, the speaker who presents himself or herself as plain folks often is not. And even if he or she is plain folks, it has nothing to do with the issue under discussion.
- **Card-stacking.** In the pseudo-argument known as card-stacking, the speaker selects only evidence and arguments that support his or her case and may even falsify evidence or distort facts to better fit the case. Despite these misrepresentations, the speaker presents the supporting materials as "fair" and "impartial."
- **Thin entering wedge.** In using the thin entering wedge, a speaker argues against a proposal or new development on the grounds that it will be a "thin entering wedge" that will open the floodgates to all sorts of catastrophes. Though often based on no evidence, this argument has been used throughout

history to oppose change. Some examples are "wedge" claims that school integration and interracial marriage will bring the collapse of American education and society, same-sex unions will destroy the family, and banning smoking in all public places will lead to the collapse of the restaurant industry.

- **Agenda-setting.** In agenda-setting a speaker contends that XYZ is the issue and that all others are unimportant and insignificant. This kind of fallacious appeal is heard frequently, as in "Balancing the budget is the key to the city's survival" or "There's only one issue confronting elementary education in our largest cities, and that is violence." In almost all situations, however, there are many issues and many sides to each issue. Often the person proclaiming that X is the issue really means, "I'll be able to persuade you if you focus solely on X and ignore the other issues."

Listening at the Evaluation Stage. Once you've received, understood, and have the message in memory, you need to evaluate it. After all, not all messages are equal—some are lies, some are truths; some are significant, some are trivial; some are constructive, some are destructive. In evaluating messages consider these strategies:

- **Resist evaluation until you fully understand the speaker's point of view.** This is not always easy, but it's always essential. If you put a label on what the speaker is saying (ultraconservative, bleeding-heart liberal), you'll hear the remainder of the messages through these labels.
- **Distinguish facts from opinions and personal interpretations by the speaker.** And, most important, fix these labels in mind with the information; for example, try

to remember that Jesse thinks Pat did XYZ, not just that Pat did XYZ.

- **Identify any biases, self-interests, or prejudices that may lead the speaker to slant unfairly what is said.** It's often wise to ask if the material is being presented fairly or if this person is slanting it in some way.
- **Look for logical reasoning.** Too often speakers will appear to use logic but on closer examination it is just a smoke screen. For more on this see the & Box, Reasoning Fallacies.

Listening at the Responding Stage. After you evaluate the message, you're likely to respond in some way. And, of course, a speaker generally expects a response. Here are just a few strategies for improving your responding to another's messages:

- **Support the speaker throughout.** Give the speaker listening cues, such as head nods and minimal responses such as "I see" or "mm-hmm." Using the "like" icon, poking back, retweeting, and commenting on another's photos or posts will also prove supportive.
- **Own your responses.** Take responsibility for what you say. Instead of saying, "Nobody will want to do that" say something like "I don't want to do that." Use the anonymity that most social networks allow with discretion.
- **Resist solving the person's problem.** Avoid responding to another's feelings" with "solving the person's problems" (as men are often accused of doing) unless, of course, you're asked for advice. Oftentimes, people simply want to vent and just want you to hear what they have to say.
- **Focus on the other person.** Avoid multitasking when you're listening. Show the speaker that he or she is your primary focus. You can't be a supportive listener, if you're also listening to a CD, so take off the headphones; shut

down the Smartphone and the television; turn away from the computer screen. And, instead of looking around the room, look at the speaker; the speaker's eyes should be your main focus.

- **Avoid being a thought-completing listener who listens a little and then finishes the speaker's thought.** This is especially inappropriate when listening to someone who might stutter or have word-finding difficulties. Instead, express respect (and a real willingness to listen) by giving the speaker time to complete his or her thoughts. Completing someone's thoughts often communicates the message that nothing important is going to be said ("I already know it").

Try It

Try using these strategies one stage at a time. For example, the next time you attend a meeting, consciously use the strategies for receiving messages. The next time, consciously apply the strategies for understanding, and so on. In short time you'll improve your overall listening significantly.

Strategies for

Listening Actively

One of the most important communication skills you can learn is that of active listening. Active listening owes its development to Thomas Gordon in his *Parent Effectiveness Training.* Active listening is a process of sending back to the speaker what you as a listener think the speaker meant—both in content and in feelings. Active listening, then, is not merely repeating the speaker's exact words, but rather putting together your understanding of the speaker's total message into a meaningful whole.

Active listening helps you as a listener to check your understanding of what the speaker said and, more important, of what he or she meant. Reflecting back perceived meanings to the speaker gives the speaker an opportunity to offer clarification and to correct any misunderstandings. Active listening also lets the speaker know that you acknowledge and accept his or her feelings.

Three simple strategies will prove useful as you learn to practice active listening: Paraphrase the speaker's meaning, express understanding, and ask questions.

- Paraphrase the speaker's meaning. Stating in your own words what you think the speaker means and feels helps ensure understanding and also shows interest in the speaker. Paraphrasing gives the speaker a chance to extend what was originally said. Thus, when Suzanne echoes your thoughts, you're given the opportunity to elaborate on why rewriting the budget report means so much to you. In paraphrasing, be objective; be especially careful not to lead the speaker in the direction you think he or she should go. Also, be careful that you don't overdo paraphrase; only a very small percentage of statements need paraphrasing. Paraphrase when you feel there's a chance for misunderstanding or when you want to express support for the other person and keep the conversation going.

- Express understanding of the speaker's feelings. Echo the feelings the speaker expressed or implied ("You must have felt horrible"). This expression of empathy will help you further check your perception of the speaker's feelings. This will also allow the speaker to see his or her feelings more objectively (especially helpful when these are feelings of anger, hurt, or depression) and to elaborate on them. In communicating your understanding back to the person, be especially careful to avoid sending "solution messages"; see the & Box, Active Listening Cautions.

Active Listening Cautions

In listening actively, be sure to avoid solution messages which tell the person how he or she should feel or what he or she should do. Four types of messages send solutions, and you'll want to avoid them in your active listening:

- **Ordering messages:** "Do this . . . ." "Don't touch that . . . ."
- **Warning and threatening messages:** "If you don't do this, you'll . . . ." "If you do that, you'll . . . ."
- **Preaching and moralizing messages:** "People should all . . . ." "We all have responsibilities . . . ."
- **Advising messages:** "Why don't you . . . ." "I think you should . . . ."

- **Ask questions.** Asking questions ensures your own understanding of the speaker's thoughts and feelings and secures additional information ("How did you feel when you read your job appraisal report?"). Ask questions to provide just enough stimulation and support for the speaker to feel he or she can elaborate on these thoughts and feelings. These questions will further confirm your interest and concern for the speaker but not pry into unrelated areas or challenge the speaker in any way.

Try It

Try active listening but do it subtly. Too obvious attempts will likely be perceived as phony.

Strategies for

Lying Detection

Lying is the act of (1) sending messages (2) with the intention of giving another person information you believe to be false, and (3) when that person expects you to tell the truth.

1. Lying involves the sending of some kind of verbal and/or nonverbal message and its reception by another person.
2. The message must be sent to intentionally deceive. If you give false information to someone but you believe it to be true, then you haven't lied. You do lie when you communicate information that you believe to be untrue and you intend to mislead the other person.
3. The person must expect you to be telling the truth. For example, the poker player who bluffs—trying to deceive the others at the table into thinking he or she had a winning hand—is not lying because the people playing poker expect you to attempt deception; it's part of the game.

How People Lie

Here are some of the ways people lie.

- **Exaggeration**. Here you lead people to believe that, for example, you earn more money than you do or that your grades are better than they are, or that your relationship is more satisfying than it really is.
- **Minimization**. Instead of exaggerating the facts, here you minimize them. You can minimize your lack of money (we have more than enough), the importance of poor grades, or your relationship dissatisfaction.
- **Substitution**. In this method you exchange the truth for a lie—for example, *I wasn't at the bar, I stopped in at Starbucks for coffee.*
- **Equivocation**. When you equivocate, your message is sufficiently ambiguous to lead people to think something different from your intention. *That outfit really is something, very interesting* instead of *Ugh!*
- **Omission**. And of course you can lie by not sending certain messages. So, when your romantic partner asks where you were last night, you might omit those things your partner would frown on and just include the positives.

One of the more interesting questions about lying is how do liars act. Do they act differently from those telling the truth? And, if they do act differently, how can you tell when someone is lying to you? These questions are not easy to answer and we are far from having complete answers to such questions. But, we have learned a great deal. Before reading what research has found, consider these cautions.

None of the behaviors to be discussed, taken alone or in a group, is proof that a person is lying. Liars can be especially adept at learning to hide any signs that they might be lying. Nor is an absence of these features proof that the person is telling the truth.

It's very difficult to detect when a person is lying and when telling the truth. The hundreds of research studies conducted on this topic find that in most instances people judge lying accurately in less than 60% of the cases, only slightly better than chance. And these percentages are even lower when you try to detect lying in a person from a culture very different from your own.

Another reason that makes lie detection so difficult in close relationships is that the liar knows how to lie, largely because he or she knows how you think and can therefore tailor lies that you'll fall for. And, of course, the liar often has considerable time to rehearse the lie which generally makes lying more convincing and more difficult to detect. To complicate things just a bit further: Lie detection, as you'd expect, is more difficult in *inter*cultural situations than in *intra*cultural situations.

With these cautions in mind, and from a combination of research studies, the following strategies should help you in detecting lying:

- **Look for evidence that the person is holding back.** Liars often hold back. They speak more slowly (perhaps to monitor what they're saying), take longer to respond to questions (again, perhaps monitoring their messages), and generally give less information and elaboration.

- **Look for leaks.** Liars leak. Very slight facial and eye movements may reveal the person's real feelings, a process referred to as leakage. Often this is the result of what has come to be called "duping delight"—the pleasure you get when you feel you're putting over a lie. Here you may leak your lying through slight movements in your lips or eyes.

- **Beware of biases.** There is some evidence to show that lie detection is even more difficult (that is, less accurate) in long-standing romantic relationships—the very relationships in which the most significant lying occurs. One of the most important reasons for this is the truth bias. In most situations you assume that the person is telling the truth; you normally operate under the principle which assumes that what a person says is the truth. This truth bias is especially strong in long-term relationships where it's simply expected that each person tells the truth. There are also situations where there is a deception bias. For example, in prison where lying is so prevalent and where lie detection is a crucial survival skill, prisoners often operate with a lie bias and assume that what the speaker is saying is a lie.

- **Look for illogical connections**. Liars make less sense. Liar's messages contain more discrepancies; more inconsistencies.

- **Look for uncooperative behavior**. Liars give a more negative impression. Generally, liars are seen as less willing to be cooperative, smile less than truth-tellers, and are more defensive.

- **Look at body tension**. Liars are tense. The tension may be revealed by their higher pitched voices and their excessive body movements.

- **Look at pupil dilation**. Liars exhibit greater pupil dilation and more eye blinks; more gaze aversion

- **Look for variations in pitch.** Liars speak with a higher vocal pitch; voices sound as if they were under stress

- **Look for errors and hesitations**. Liars make more errors and use more hesitations in their speech; they pause more and for longer periods of time;

- **Look at hand and leg movements**. Liars make more hand, leg, and foot movements

- **Look for self-touching movements**. Liars engage in more self-touching movements, for example, touching their face or hair, and more object touching, for example, playing with a coffee cup or pen

- **Use a baseline.** Interpret your findings in light of a baseline for the person's normal behavior. If the person is usually or often tense, for example, then the level of tension to signal possible lying would need to be much higher than for someone who is normally calm and relaxed.

Try It

In detecting lying be especially careful that you formulate any conclusions with a clear understanding that you can be wrong and that accusations of lying (especially when untrue but even when true) can often damage a relationship to the point where it's beyond repair. Because the accusation that someone is lying is such serious business it's probably a lot safer to practice you lie detection skills from afar—while watching a crime show or some politician claim innocence in the face of accusations to the contrary.

Strategies for

Metacommunicating

Verbal messages may refer to the objects and things in the world (in what is called *object language)* but also to itself—you can talk about your talk, write about your writing (in what is called *metacommunication*). The prefix *meta-* can mean a variety of things, but as used in communication, philosophy, and psychology, its meaning is best translated as *about.* Thus, *metacommunication* is communication *about* communication, *metalanguage* is language *about* language, and a *metamessage* is a message *about* a message.

Actually, you use this distinction every day, perhaps without realizing it. For example, when you send someone an e-mail with a seemingly sarcastic comment and then put a smiley at the end, the smiley communicates about your communication; it says something like "this message is not to be taken literally; I'm trying to be humorous." The smiley is a metamessage; it's a message about a message. When you say, in preface to some comment, "I'm not sure about this, but . . . ," you're communicating a message about a message; you're commenting on the message and asking that it be understood with the qualification that you may be wrong. When you conclude a comment with "I'm only kidding," you're metacommunicating; you're communicating about your communication. In relationship communication you often talk in metalanguage and say things like, "We really need to talk about the way we communicate when we're out with company" or, "You're too critical" or, "I love when you tell me how much you love me." And, of course, you can also use nonverbal messages to metacommunicate. You can wink at someone to indicate that you're only kidding or sneer after saying "Yeah, that was great," with the sneer contradicting the literal meaning of the verbal message.

Here are a few strategies for increasing your metacommunication effectiveness:

- **Explain your feelings.** It helps if you can include your feelings as well as your thoughts. For more on this see the *Emotional Expression* chapter.
- **Give clear feedforward.** This will help the other person get a general picture of the messages that will follow.
- **Paraphrase.** It often helps, especially with complex messages, to paraphrase so as to make your meaning extra clear. Similarly, check on your understanding of another's message by paraphrasing what you think the other person means.
- **Ask for clarification.** If you have doubts about another's meaning ask for clarification.
- **Use metacommunication to talk about your talk.** Metacommunication is especially important when you want to clarify the communication patterns between yourself and another person: "I'd like to talk about the way you talk about me to our friends" or, "I think we should talk about the way we talk about sex."

Try It

Analyze your own use of metacommunication. In what ways do you normally metacommunicate? Are these generally productive? What kinds of metacommunication messages do you wish other people would use more often?

Strategies for

Mindfulness

Mindfulness is a state of mental awareness; in a mindful state you're conscious of your reasons for thinking or communicating in a particular way. And, especially important in all forms of communication, you become aware of your choices. You act with an awareness of your available choices. Its opposite, mindlessness, is a lack of conscious awareness of your thinking or communicating. To apply communication skills appropriately and effectively, you need to be mindful of the unique communication situation you're in, of your available communication options or choices, and of the reasons why one option is likely to prove better than the others. You can look at this book as one means of awakening your mindfulness about the way you can use communication strategically. To increase mindfulness in general, try the following strategies:

- **Create and recreate categories**. Learn to see objects, events, and people as belonging to a wide variety of categories. Try to see, for example, your prospective romantic partner in a variety of roles——child, parent, employee, neighbor, friend, financial contributor, and so on. Avoid storing in memory an image of a person with only one specific label; if you do, you'll find it difficult to re-categorize the person later.

- **Be open to new information and points of view.** Be open even when these contradict your most firmly held stereotypes. New information forces you to reconsider what might be outmoded ways of thinking. New information can help you challenge long-held but now inappropriate beliefs and attitudes. Be willing to see your own and others' behaviors from a variety of viewpoints, especially from the perspective of people very different from yourself.

- **Beware of relying too heavily on first impressions.** Treat your first impressions as tentative——as hypotheses that need further investigation. Be prepared to revise, reject, or accept these initial impressions.

- **Consider the possibility of misinterpretation.** Regardless of what piece of information you're looking at and deciphering, there is a possibility for misinterpretation. Can the message be misinterpreted? What can you do to make sure it's interpreted correctly? For example, you can paraphrase or restate the message in different ways or you can ask the person to paraphrase.

- **Focus on the uniqueness of the situation.** Remind yourself of what you already know about a situation, recall that all communication situations are different, and ask yourself how you can best adapt your messages to this unique situation. For example, you may want to be especially positive to a friend who is depressed but not so positive to someone who betrayed a confidence.

- **Pause and think.** Think before you act. Especially in delicate situations (for example, when expressing anger or when conveying commitment messages), it's wise to pause and think over the situation mindfully. In this way you'll stand a better chance of acting and reacting appropriately.

Try It

Try thinking mindfully about the next problem presented to you. Go through each of the strategies mindfully.

Strategies for

Perceptual Accuracy

Successful communication depends in large part on the accuracy of the impressions you form of others. Here are a few strategies to increase your accuracy in impression formation.

- **Analyze impressions**. Subject your perceptions to logical analysis, to critical thinking. For example:
    - Recognize your own role in perception. Your emotional and physiological state will influence the meaning you give to your perceptions. A movie may seem hysterically funny when you're in a good mood, but just plain stupid when you're in a bad mood.
    - Avoid early conclusions. Formulate hypotheses to test against additional information and evidence (rather than conclusions). Look for a variety of cues pointing in the same direction. The more cues that point to the same conclusion, the more likely your conclusion will be correct. Be especially alert to contradictory cues that seem to refute your initial hypotheses. At the same time, seek validation from others. Do others see things in the same way you do? If not, ask yourself if your perceptions may be distorted in some way.

- **Check perceptions**. Perception checking will help you lessen your chances of misinterpreting another's feelings and will also give the other person an opportunity to elaborate on his or her thoughts and feelings. In its most basic form, perception checking consists of two steps.

- Describe what you see or hear. Try to do this as descriptively (not evaluatively) as you can. Sometimes you may wish to offer several possibilities, for example, "You've called me from work a lot this week. You seem concerned that everything is all right at home" or "You've not wanted to talk with me all week. You say that my work is fine but you don't seem to want to give me the same responsibilities that other editorial assistants have."
- Seek confirmation. Ask the other person if your description is accurate. Avoid mind reading. Don't try to read the thoughts and feelings of another person just from observing their behaviors. Avoid phrasing your questions defensively, as in "You really don't want to go out, do you? I knew you didn't when you turned on the television." Instead, ask supportively, for example, "Would you rather watch TV"? or "Are you worried about the kids?" or "Are you displeased with my work? Is there anything I can do to improve my job performance?"

- **Reduce uncertainty.** In every communication situation, there is some degree of ambiguity. There are a variety of uncertainty reduction strategies.
  - Observe. Observing another person while he or she is engaged in an active task, preferably interacting with others in an informal social situation, will often reveal a great deal about the person, as people are less apt to monitor their behaviors and more likely to reveal their true selves in informal situations.

    - Ask others. Learn about a person through asking others. You might inquire of a colleague if a third person finds you interesting and might like to have dinner with you.
    - Interact with the individual. For example, you can ask questions: "Do you enjoy sports?" "What did you think of that computer science course?" "What would you do if you got fired?" You also gain knowledge of another by disclosing information about yourself. These disclosures help to create an environment that encourages disclosures from the person about whom you wish to learn more.

- **Increase cultural sensitivity**. Recognizing and being sensitive to cultural differences will help increase your accuracy in perception. For example, Russian or Chinese artists such as ballet dancers will often applaud their audience by clapping. Americans seeing this may easily interpret this as egotistical. Similarly, a German man will enter a restaurant before the woman in order to see if the place is respectable enough for the woman to enter. This simple custom can easily be interpreted as rude when viewed by people from cultures in which it's considered courteous for the woman to enter first.

  Cultural sensitivity will help counteract the difficulty most people have in understanding the nonverbal messages of people from other cultures. For example, it's easier to interpret the facial expressions of members of your own culture than those of members of other cultures. This "in-group advantage" will assist your perceptual accuracy for members of your own culture but may hinder your accuracy for members of other cultures.

  Within every cultural group there are wide and important differences. As all Americans are not alike, neither are all Indonesians, Greeks, or Mexicans. When you make assumptions that all people of a certain culture are alike, you're thinking in stereotypes. Recognizing differences between another culture and your own, and among members of the same culture, will help you perceive people and situations more accurately.

Try It

The next time you make a judgment about another person, consciously reflect on these strategies. Does the application of these strategies alter your perceptions?

Strategies for

Politeness in Conversation

Not surprisingly, conversation is expected (at least in many cases) to follow the principle of politeness. Six maxims of politeness have been identified and seem to encompass a great deal of what we commonly think of as conversational politeness. Before reading about these maxims respond to the following statements to help you personalize the material that follows.

For each of the statements below indicate how closely they describe your typical communication. Avoid giving responses that you feel might be considered "socially acceptable." Instead, give responses that accurately represent your typical communication behavior. Use a 10-point scale, with 10 being "very accurate description of my typical conversation" and 1 being "very inaccurate description of my typical conversation."

_____ 1. I tend not to ask others to do something or to otherwise impose on others.

_____ 2. I tend to put others first, before myself.

_____ 3. I maximize the expression of approval of others and minimize any disapproval.

_____ 4. I seldom praise myself but often praise others.

_____ 5. I maximize the expression of agreement and minimize disagreement.

_____ 6. I maximize my sympathy for another and minimize any feelings of antipathy.

All six statements would characterize politeness; high numbers, say 8s, 9s, and 10s, would indicate politeness whereas low numbers, say 1s, 2s, and 3s, would indicate impoliteness. Here are the conversational politeness strategies:

- **Follow the maxim of tact (Statement 1).** Tact helps to maintain the other's autonomy (what is referred to earlier as negative face). Tact in your conversation would mean that you do not impose on others or challenge their right to do as they wish. For example, if you wanted to ask someone a favor, using the maxim of tact, you might say something like, "I know you're very busy but . . ." or "I don't mean to impose, but . . ." Not using the maxim of tact, you might say something like, "You have to lend me your car this weekend" or "I'm going to need your ATM card."
- **Follow the maxim of generosity (Statement 2).** This helps to confirm the other person's importance--the importance of the person's time, insight, or talent, for example. Using the maxim of generosity, you might say, "I'll walk the dog; I see you're busy" and violating the maxim, you might say, "I'm really busy, why don't you walk the dog; you're not doing anything important."
- **Follow the maxim of approbation (Statement 3).** Praise someone or compliment the person in some way (for example, "I was really moved by your poem") and minimizing any expression of criticism or disapproval (for example, "For a first effort, that poem wasn't half bad").
- **Follow the maxim of modesty (Statement 4).** Minimize any praise or compliments *you* might receive. At the same time, you might praise and compliment the other person. For example, using this maxim you might say something like, "Well, thank you, but I couldn't have done this without your input; that was the crucial element." Violating this maxim, you might say, "Yes, thank you, it was one of my best efforts, I have to admit."
- **Follow the maxim of agreement (Statement 5).** This refers to your seeking out areas of agreement and expressing them ("That color you selected was just right; it makes the room exciting") and at the same time to avoid and not express (or at least minimize) disagreements ("It's an interesting

choice, very different"). In violation of this maxim, you might say "That color—how can you stand it?"

- **Follow the maxim of sympathy (Statement 6).** Express understanding, sympathy, empathy, supportiveness, and the like for the other person. Using this maxim you might say, "I understand your feelings; I'm so sorry." If you violated this maxim you might say, for example, "You're making a fuss over nothing" or "You get upset over the least little thing; what is it this time?"

Try It

Personalize these maxims with examples from your own interactions and try to identify specific examples and situations in which increased politeness might have been more effective.

Strategies for

Politeness Online

The Internet has very specific rules for politeness, called netiquette or in the case of Twitter, twittiquette. Much as the rules of etiquette provide guidance in communicating in face-to-face social situations, the rules of netiquette and twittiquette provide guidance for communicating politely online. These rules not only make online communication more pleasant and easier but also improve your personal efficiency. Here are some strategies for communicating politely online.

- **Familiarize yourself with the site before contributing.** Before asking questions about the system, read the Frequently Asked Questions (FAQs). Your question has probably been asked before and you'll put less strain on the system. Lurk before speaking; read posted notices and conversations before you contribute anything yourself. Observe the kinds of photos posted and the language used. Lurking (which, in online communication is good) will help you learn the rules of the particular group and will help you avoid saying things you'd like to take back.

- **Be brief.** Communicate only the information that is needed; communicate clearly, briefly, and in an organized way. Don't over-tweet. Communicate when you have something to say; not every one of your thoughts is worth a tweet or Facebook post. The same is true of photos; not everyone wants to see 27 photos of your cat.

- **Be gentle.** Refuse a request for friendship gently or ignore it. There's no need to go into great detail about why you don't want to be friends with this person. And if you're refused, don't ask for reasons. Social networkers consider it impolite to ask for reasons why your request is refused.

- **Don't shout.** WRITING IN CAPS IS PERCEIVED AS SHOUTING. It's okay to use caps occasionally to achieve emphasis. But, it's generally preferred to give emphasis _like this_ or *like this*.

- **Be discrete.** Don't use social networking information outside the network. It's considered inappropriate and impolite to relay information that you find on Facebook, for example, to those who are not also friends with the person talked about (and who therefore would not have access to the same information about the person that you do).

- **Don't spam or flame.** Don't send unsolicited mail, repeatedly send the same mail, or post the same message (or irrelevant messages) to lots of newsgroups. Don't make personal attacks on other users. As in face-to-face conflict, personal attacks are best avoided on the Internet.

- **Avoid offensive language.** Refrain from expressions that would be considered offensive to others, such as sexist or racist terms. As you may know, software is available that will scan your e-mail, alert you if you may have broken an organizational rule, and give you a chance to revise your potentially offensive e-mail. This suggestion is especially important when you write on someone's wall in, say, Facebook or post an unflattering photo for all to see.

- **Be considerate.** Avoid asking to be friends with someone you suspect may have reason for not wanting to admit you.

For example, your supervisor may not want you to see her or his profile; if you ask, you put your supervisor in an awkward position. In this case, you might use indirect messages; for example, you might say that you want to expand your networking to work colleagues and see how your supervisor responds.

- **Don't advertise.** Don't market a product, yourself, or your services on Twitter; it's permissible on Facebook but do it discretely. And don't respond to blog posts by posting advertisements masquerading as comments. If you want to advertise, it's better to direct readers to another site; say, a blog or website.

- **Don't plagiarize.** Give credit to others for the ideas you post and certainly any direct quotations.

- **Don't brag.** Social networking's norm is modesty, at least as most social networkers think about it. So, don't brag, for example, about the number of followers you have or the number of friends. Although Facebook and Twitter identify the number of followers/friends you have, it's the website that is posting the number of followers rather than you.

Try It

Check over a few of your recent emails or social network posts for the politeness strategies identified here. Could you have followed these strategies more effectively?

Strategies for

Power

Power is the ability of one person to influence what another person thinks or does. You have power over another person to the extent that you can influence what this person thinks or what this person does. And, conversely, another person has power over you to the extent that he or she can influence what you think or do. Perhaps the most important aspect of power to recognize is that *power is asymmetrical*: If one person has greater power, the other person must have less. If you are stronger than another person, then this person is weaker than you. If you are richer, then the other person must be poorer. In any one area—for example, strength or financial wealth—one person has more and, inevitably and by definition, the other person has less (is weaker or poorer). The varied types of power are identified in the & Box, Types of Power.

&

Types of Power

Six types of power are especially important to understand: legitimate, referent, reward, coercive, expert, and information or persuasion.

- You hold **legitimate power** when others believe you have a right—by virtue of your position—to influence or control others' behaviors. For example, as an employer, judge, manager, or police officer, you'd have legitimate power by virtue of your role.

- You have **referent power** when others wish to be like you. Referent power holders often are attractive, have considerable prestige, and are well liked and well respected. For example, you may have referent power over a younger brother because he wants to be like you.
- You have **reward power** when you control the rewards that others want. Rewards may be material (money, promotion, jewelry) or social (love, friendship, respect). For example, teachers have reward power over students because they control grades, letters of recommendation, and social approval.
- You have **coercive power** when you have the ability to administer punishments to or remove rewards from others if they do not do as you wish. Usually, people who have reward power also have coercive power. For example, teachers may give poor grades or withhold recommendations. But be careful: Coercive power may reduce your other power bases. It can have a negative impact when used, for example, by supervisors on subordinates in business.
- You have **expert power** when others see you as having expertise or special knowledge. Your expert power increases when you're perceived as being unbiased and as having nothing personally to gain from exerting this power. For example, judges have expert power in legal matters and doctors have expert power in medical matters.

- **You have information power**—also called "persuasion power"—when others see you as having the ability to communicate logically and persuasively. For example, researchers and scientists may acquire information power because people perceive them as informed and critical thinkers.

Power can increase and decrease. Although people differ greatly in the amount of power they wield at any time and in any specific area, everyone can increase their power in some ways. You can lift weights and increase your physical power. You can learn the techniques of negotiation and increase your power in group situations. You can learn the principles of communication and increase your persuasive power. Power can also be decreased. Probably the most common way to lose power is by unsuccessfully trying to control another's behavior. For example, the person who threatens you with punishment and then fails to carry out the threat loses power. Another way to lose power is to allow others to control you; for example, to allow others to take unfair advantage of you. When you don't confront these power tactics of others, you lose power yourself.

Power follows the principle of less interest. The more a person needs a relationship, the less power that person has in it. The less a person needs a relationship, the greater is that person's power. In a love relationship, for example, the person who maintains greater power is the one who would find it easier to break up the relationship. The person who is unwilling (or unable) to break up has little power, precisely because he or she is dependent on the relationship and the rewards provided by the other person.

Power generates privilege. When one person has power over another person, the person with power is generally assumed to have certain privileges, many of which are communication privileges. And the greater the power difference, the greater is the license of the more powerful individual. Sometimes we're mindful of the privilege or license that comes with power. Most often, however, we seem to operate mindlessly, with no one questioning the power structure. For example, those with power may encroach on the territory of those with little power (a supervisor can enter the cubicle of a trainee but the trainee cannot enter the office of the supervisor—at least not without being invited or before knocking). Similarly, a supervisor may touch the arm or rearrange the collar of a subordinate, but not the other way around. The general may touch the corporal, but not the other way around. The doctor may put his or her arm on a patient, but the patient would not do that to a doctor.

Here are some strategies for communicating power nonverbally.

- **Avoid adaptors.** Adaptors are touching movements of the self (playing with your hair or rubbing your nose), of others (removing a speck of dust from someone's cheek), or of objects (poking holes in the Styrofoam coffee cup). Adaptors may make you appear uncomfortable and hence without power. Avoid these especially when you wish to communicate confidence and control.

- **Use consistent packaging.** Be especially careful that your verbal and nonverbal messages don't contradict each other. Each will weaken the other.

- **Use facial expressions and gestures as appropriate.** These help you express your concern for the other person as well as your comfort and control of the communication situation. Smile to show approval and that you're enjoying yourself but avoid excessive or purposeless smiling.

- **Select the right chairs.** When sitting, select chairs you can get in and out of easily; avoid deep plush chairs that you will sink into and will have trouble getting out of.

- **Shake.** To communicate confidence with your handshake, exert more pressure than usual and hold the grip a bit longer than normal.

- **Dress conservatively**. Other things being equal, dress relatively conservatively if you want to influence others; conservative clothing is usually associated with power and status. Trendy and fad clothing usually communicates a lack of power and status. And, of course, expensive clothing is more powerful than inexpensive clothing.

- **Walk and gesture slowly and purposefully.** To appear hurried is to appear as without power, as if you were rushing to meet the expectations of another person who had power over you. Avoid gestures and movements that can appear random and without purpose. This will generally signal discomfort.

- **Maintain eye contact.** People who maintain eye contact are judged to be more at ease and less afraid to engage in meaningful interaction than those who avoid eye contact. (Be aware, however, that in some contexts, if you use excessive or protracted direct eye contact, you may be seen as exercising coercive power. When you break eye contact, direct your gaze downward; otherwise you'll communicate a lack of interest in the other person.

- **Avoid vocalized pauses.** Avoid the "ers" and "ahs" that frequently punctuate conversations when you're not quite sure of what to say next.

- **Maintain reasonably close distances between yourself and those with whom you interact.** If the distance is too far, you may be seen as fearful or uninvolved. If the distance is too close, you may be seen as pushy or overly aggressive.

- **Relax.** A relaxed posture communicates confidence and control—qualities of power. A tense body posture can easily signal fear and discomfort—qualities of the powerless.

- **Vary your speech rate, volume, and pitch as appropriate to the conversation.** Be careful to avoid a monotone speaking style.

- **Take up your space.** If you crouch in the corner of a couch, for example, you're going to appear less powerful than if you take up your allotted space. If you take up too much space, for example, spreading your legs apart and in effect taking up two spaces, you're likely to be seen as impolite.

- **Still your feet.** Excessive foot movement usually signals a discomfort and hence little power.

Here are a few verbal strategies:

- **Avoid hesitations.** Avoid the all too common, for example, "I *er* want to say that *ah* this one is *er* the best, *you know*?" Hesitations make you sound unprepared and uncertain.

- **Avoid too many intensifiers.** Intensifiers are fine in moderation; overused, they are likely to decrease your power. Avoid, for example, statements like these: "Really, this was the greatest; it was truly phenomenal." Too many intensifiers make everything sound the same and don't allow you to intensify what should be emphasized.

- **Avoid disqualifiers.** When you disqualify yourself you detract from your credibility and hence power. Avoid, for example, statements like "I didn't read the entire article, but . . ." or "I didn't actually see the accident, but. . . ." Disqualifiers signal a lack of competence and a feeling of uncertainty.

- **Avoid tag questions.** Avoid, for example, statements such as *That was a great movie, wasn't it? She's brilliant, don't you thin*k? Tag questions ask for another's agreement and therefore may signal your need for agreement and your own uncertainty.

- **Avoid self-critical statements.** When you criticize yourself and say, for example, "I'm not very good at this" or "This is my first interview" you're just calling attention to your lack of power. Self-critical statements signal a lack of confidence and may make public your own inadequacies.

- **Avoid slang and vulgar expressions.** Slang and vulgarity signal low social class and hence little power.

Try It

Begin to incorporate one or two or three of these strategies into your own communications as you think appropriate. Avoid using too many too quickly; they're likely to backfire.

Strategies for

Relationship Development

Here are some examples of how people communicate as they develop and seek to maintain their relationships, presented in the form of strategies for more effective interpersonal relationships. The strategies are the same whether the interaction is face-to-face or online (through e-mail, Facebook postings, instant messaging, texting, and tweeting).

- **Be nice.** Researchers call this prosocial behavior. Be polite, cheerful, and friendly; avoid criticism. Compromise even when it involves self-sacrifice. Prosocial behavior also includes talking about a shared future; for example, talking about a future vacation or buying a house together as well as acting affectionately and romantically.

- **Communicate.** Call or text just to say, "How are you?" or send cards or letters. Sometimes communication is merely "small talk" that is insignificant in itself but is engaged in because it preserves contact. Also included here would be talking about the positive aspects of the relationship and talking about shared feelings. Responding constructively in a conflict (even when your partner may act in ways harmful to the relationship) is another strategy.

- **Be open.** Engage in direct discussion and listen to the other—for example, self-disclose, talk about what you want from the relationship, give advice (when asked for), and express empathy.

- **Give assurances**. Assure the other person of the significance of the relationship—for example, comfort the other, put your partner first, and express love.

- **Share joint activities.** Spend time with the other—for example, playing ball, visiting mutual friends, doing specific things as a couple (even cleaning the house), and sometimes just being together and talking with no concern for what is done. Controlling (eliminating or reducing) extra-relational activities would be another type of togetherness behavior. Also included here would be ceremonial behaviors; for example, celebrating birthdays and anniversaries, discussing past pleasurable times, and eating at a favorite restaurant.

- **Be positive.** Try to make interactions pleasant and upbeat—for example, holding hands, giving in to make your partner happy, and doing favors. At the same time, you would avoid those issues that might cause arguments.

- **Focus on improving yourself.** Work on making yourself look especially good and attractive to the other person.

- **Be empathic.** Let the other person know that you can feel what he or she feels, at least to some extent. For more on this see the *Empathy* chapter.

Try It

Recall a recent interaction with someone you wanted to get to know better. Try to identify the strategies you used; very likely you used some of those discussed here. More important, which didn't you use but could have?

Strategies for

Relationship Deterioration

Like communication in developing relationships, communication in deteriorating relationships involves special patterns and special strategies. These patterns are in part a response to the deterioration; you communicate the way you do because you feel that your relationship is in trouble. However, these patterns are also causative: The communication patterns you use largely determine the fate of your relationship. Here are a few communication strategies that are seen during relationship deterioration—use them or avoid them as the specific situation warrants.

- **Withdraw.** Nonverbally, withdrawal is seen in the greater space you need and in the speed with which tempers and other signs of disturbance arise when that space is invaded. Other nonverbal signs of withdrawal include a decrease in eye contact and touching; less similarity in clothing; and fewer displays of items associated with the other person, such as bracelets, photographs, and rings. Verbally, withdrawal is marked by a decreased desire to talk and especially to listen. At times, you may use small talk not as a preliminary to serious conversation but as an alternative, perhaps to avoid confronting the serious issues.

- **Reduce self-disclosure.** Self-disclosing communications decline significantly. If the relationship is dying, you may think self-disclosure not worth the effort. Or you may limit your self-disclosures because you feel that the other person may not accept them or can no longer be trusted to be supportive and empathic.

- **Deception increases as relationships break down.** Sometimes this takes the form of clear-cut lies, which you or your partner may use to avoid arguments over such things as staying out all night, not calling, or being seen in the wrong place with the wrong person. At other times, lies may be used because of a feeling of shame; you may not want the other person to think less of you. One of the problems with deception is that it has a way of escalating, eventually creating a climate of distrust and disbelief.

- **Decrease positive and increase negative messages.** During deterioration there's an increase in negative and a decrease in positive messages. Whereas once you praised the other's behaviors, now you criticize them. Often the behaviors have not changed significantly; what has changed is your way of looking at them. What once was a cute habit now becomes annoying; what once was "different" now becomes inconsiderate. When a relationship is deteriorating, requests for pleasurable behaviors decrease ("Will you fix me my favorite dessert?") and requests to stop unpleasant or negative behaviors increase ("Will you stop monopolizing the phone?"). Even the social niceties that accompany requests get lost as they deteriorate from "Would you please make me a cup of coffee, honey?" to "Get me some coffee, will you?" to "Where's my coffee?"

Try It

Perhaps the best way to become familiar with the strategies of disengagement is to listen to those who have gone through it. Very likely you'll be able to pick out the logical and reasonable strategies from those that just make the situation worse.

Strategies for

Relationship Dissolution

Regardless of the specific reason for the end of the relationship, relationship breakups are difficult to deal with; invariably they cause stress and emotional problems, and they may actually create as much pain in a person's brain as physical injuries. Women, it seems, experience even greater depression and social dysfunction than men after relationship dissolution. Consequently, it's important to give attention to self-repair. Here are a few strategies to ease the difficulty that is sure to be experienced, whether the breakup is between friends or lovers or occurs because of death, separation, or the loss of affection and connection.

- **Break the loneliness-depression cycle.** Instead of wallowing in loneliness and depression, be active, do things. Engage in social activities with friends and others in your support system. Many people feel they should bear their burdens alone. Men, in particular, have been taught that this is the only "manly" way to handle things. But seeking the support of others is one of the best antidotes to the unhappiness caused when a relationship ends. Tell your friends and family of your situation—in only general terms, if you prefer—and make it clear that you want support. Seek out people who are positive and nurturing. Avoid negative individuals who will paint the world in even darker tones. Make the distinction between seeking support and seeking advice. If you feel you need advice, you may want to seek out a professional.

- **Take time out.** Resist the temptation to jump into a new relationship while the old one is still warm or before a new one can be assessed with some objectivity. At the same time, resist swearing off all relationships. Neither extreme works well. Take time out for yourself. Renew your relationship with yourself. If you were in a long-term relationship, you probably saw yourself as part of a team, as part of a couple. Now get to know yourself as a unique individual, standing alone at present but fully capable of entering a meaningful relationship in the near future.

- **Bolster your self-esteem.** When relationships fail, self-esteem often declines. This seems especially true for those who did not initiate the breakup. You may feel guilty for having caused the breakup or inadequate for not holding on to the relationship. You may feel unwanted and unloved. Your task is to regain a positive self-image. Recognize, too, that having been in a relationship that failed—even if you view yourself as the main cause of the breakup—does not mean that you are a failure. Neither does it mean that you cannot succeed in a new and different relationship. It does mean that something went wrong with this one relationship. Ideally, it was a failure from which you have learned something important about yourself and about your relationship behavior.

- **Remove or avoid uncomfortable relationship symbols.** After any breakup, there are a variety of reminders—photographs, gifts, and letters, for example. Resist the temptation to throw these out. Instead, remove them. Give them to a friend to hold or put them in a closet where you'll not see them. If possible, avoid places you frequented together. These symbols will bring back uncomfortable memories. After you have achieved some emotional distance, you can go back and enjoy these as reminders of a once pleasant relationship.

- **Become mindful of your own relationship patterns.** Avoid repeating negative patterns. Many people repeat their mistakes. They enter second and third relationships with the same blinders, faulty preconceptions, or unrealistic expectations with which they entered earlier involvements. Instead, use the knowledge gained from your failed relationship to prevent repeating the same patterns. At the same time, don't become a prophet of doom. Don't see in every relationship vestiges of the old. Don't jump at the first conflict and say, "Here it goes all over again." Treat the new relationship as the unique relationship it is. Don't evaluate it through past experiences. Use past relationships and experiences as guides, not filters.

Try It

A good way to appreciate these strategies is to examine the breakups that you see in novels and film. Very likely at the early stages of the relationship, the characters violate the strategies noted here but in the end realize the error of their thinking and employ productive strategies such as those discussed here.

Strategies for

Relationship Repair

If you wish to save a relationship, you may try to do so by changing your communication patterns and, in effect, using the strategies identified here. We can look at repairing a relationship in terms of the following six strategies, whose first letters conveniently spell out the word *REPAIR*, a useful reminder that repair is not a one-step but a multistep process.

- **Recognize the problem** Your first step is to identify the problem and to recognize it both intellectually and emotionally. Specify what is wrong with your present relationship (in concrete terms) and what changes would be needed to make it better (again, in specific terms). Create a picture of your relationship as you want it to be, and compare that picture to the way your relationship looks now. Specify the changes that would have to take place if the ideal picture were to replace the present picture. Try also to see the problem from your partner's point of view and to have your partner see the problem from yours. Exchange these perspectives, empathically and with open minds. Try, too, to be descriptive when discussing grievances, taking special care to avoid such troublesome terms as "always" and "never." Own your feelings and thoughts; use messages that take responsibility for your feelings instead of blaming your partner.

- **Engage in productive communication and conflict resolution**. Here are several suggestions:

- Look closely for relational messages that will help clarify motivations and needs. Respond to these messages as well as to the content messages.
- Exchange perspectives and see the situation as your partner does.
- Practice empathic and positive responses, even in conflict situations.
- Remember the principle of irreversibility; think carefully before saying things you may later regret.
- Keep the channels of communication open. Be available to discuss problems, to negotiate solutions, and to practice new and more productive communication patterns.
- Similarly, the skills of effective conflict resolution are crucial in any attempt at relationship repair. For more on this see the *Conflict Management* chatper. If partners address relationship problems by deploying productive conflict resolution strategies, the difficulties may be resolved, and the relationship may actually emerge stronger and healthier. If, however, unproductive and destructive strategies are used, then the relationship may well deteriorate further.

- **Pose possible solutions**. After the problem is identified, discuss solutions—possible ways to lessen or eliminate the difficulty. Look for solutions that will enable both of you to win. Try to avoid "solutions" in which one person wins and the other loses. With such win–lose solutions, resentment and hostility are likely to fester.

- **Affirm each other.** Any strategy of relationship repair should incorporate supportiveness and positive evaluations. For example and not surprisingly, happy couples engage in greater positive behavior exchange: They communicate more agreement, approval, and positive affect than do unhappy couples. Clearly, these behaviors result from the positive feelings the partners have for each other. However, it can also be argued that these expressions help to increase the positive regard each person has for the other. One way to affirm another is to talk positively. Reverse negative communication patterns. For example, instead of withdrawing, talk about the causes of and the possible cures for your disagreements and problems. Reverse the tendency to hide your inner self. Disclose your feelings. Compliments, positive stroking, and all the nonverbals that say "I care" are especially important when you wish to reverse negative communication patterns. An interesting way of increasing mutual affirmation is with cherishing behaviors; see the & Box, Cherishing Behaviors.

Cherishing Behaviors

Cherishing behaviors are an especially insightful way to affirm another person and to increase favor exchange. **Cherishing behaviors** are those small gestures you enjoy receiving from your partner (a smile, a wink, a squeeze, a kiss). Cherishing behaviors should be (1) specific and positive, (2) focused on the present and future rather than related to issues about which the partners have argued in the past, (3) capable of being performed daily, and (4) easily executed. People can make a list of the cherishing behaviors they each wish to receive and then exchange lists. Each person then performs the cherishing behaviors desired by the partner. At first, these behaviors may seem self-conscious and awkward. In time, however, they will become a normal part of interaction.

- **Integrate solutions into normal behavior** Often solutions that are reached after an argument are followed for only a very short time; then the couple goes back to their previous, unproductive behavior patterns. Instead, integrate the solutions into your normal behavior; make them an integral part of your everyday relationship behavior. For example, make the exchange of favors, compliments, and cherishing behaviors a part of your normal relationship behavior.

- **Risk** Take risks in trying to improve your relationship. Risk giving favors without any certainty of reciprocity. Risk rejection by making the first move to make up or by saying you're sorry. Be willing to change, to adapt, and to take on new tasks and responsibilities. Risk the possibility that a significant part of the problem is you—that you're being unreasonable or controlling or stingy and that this is causing problems and needs to be changed.

Try It

Try one or two or three of these strategies when you want to repair a broken or damaged relationship or examine the repair strategies in literature or film—they are surely in every romantic novel or movie.

Strategies for

Self-Awareness

Self-awareness refers to the degree to which you know yourself. Some people are extremely self-aware—analyzing and probing every bit of behavior in an attempt to understand every action, every thought. Others are extremely lacking in self-awareness; they seem hardly to know themselves. Either extreme seems to pose problems; what seems most desirable is to have an awareness of reasonable depth, an awareness of who you are that is honest and fair. Self-awareness will enable you to see yourself more clearly, both your strengths and your weaknesses—hopefully, to capitalize on the former and repair the latter.

The Johari Window

An interesting way of looking at self-awareness is in terms of a model called the Johari Window, named for its developers, Joseph Luft and Harry Ingham. Visualize this model as a window with four panes of glass, each pane corresponds to one of your four selves:

- The open self contains all the information that you know about yourself and that others also know. . The type of information included here might range from your name, skin color, and sex to your age, political and religious affiliations, and financial situation. Your open self will vary in size depending on the

- situation you're in and the person with whom you're interacting. Some people, for example, make you feel comfortable and supported; to them, you open yourself wide, but to others you may prefer to leave most of yourself closed.

- The blind self contains all the information about you that others know but that you do not. These may include relatively insignificant habits like saying "You know," gestures like rubbing your nose when you get angry, or traits such as a distinct body odor; they also may include things as significant as defense mechanisms, fight strategies, or repressed experiences.

- The hidden self contains all that you know of yourself and of others that you keep secret. In any interaction, this area includes everything you don't want to reveal, whether it's relevant or irrelevant to the conversation. At the extremes of the hidden self spectrum, we have the over-disclosers and the under-disclosers. The over-disclosers tell all. They tell you their marital difficulties, their children's problems, their financial status, and just about everything else. The under-disclosers tell nothing. They talk about you but not about themselves.

- The unknown self represents truths about yourself that neither you nor others know. Sometimes this unknown self is revealed through temporary changes brought about by special experimental conditions such as hypnosis or sensory deprivation. Sometimes this area is revealed by certain projective tests or dreams. Mostly, however, it's revealed by the fact that you're constantly learning things about yourself that you didn't know before (things that were previously in the unknown self)—for example, that you become defensive when someone asks you a question or voices disagreement, or that you compliment others in the hope of being complimented back.

In this view, self-awareness consists of a large open self and small blind and unknown selves. Gaining in self-awareness is achieved when information is moved from the blind or unknown self to the open or hidden self.

- **Listen to others.** Conveniently, others are constantly giving you the very feedback you need to increase self-awareness. In every interaction people comment on you in some way—on what you do, what you say, how you look. Sometimes these comments are explicit: "Loosen up" or "Don't take things so hard." Often they're "hidden" in the way others look at you—in the expressionless face that indicates disagreement or disappointment or the broad smile that says, "I think you're wonderful."

- **Increase your open self.** Revealing yourself to others will help increase your self-awareness. As you talk about yourself, you may see connections that you had previously missed. With feedback from others, you may gain still more insight. By increasing your open self, you also increase the chances that others will reveal what they know about you.

- **Seek information about yourself.** Encourage people to reveal what they know about you. Use situations that arise every day to gain self-information: "Do you think I came down too hard on the kids today?" "Do you think I was assertive enough when asking for the raise?" But seek this self-awareness in moderation. If you do it too often, your friends will soon look for someone else with whom to talk.

- **Dialogue with yourself.** No one knows you better than you know yourself. Ask yourself self-awareness questions: What motivates me to act as I do? What are my short-term and long-term goals? How do I plan to achieve them? What are my strengths and weaknesses?

Try It

Try increasing your self-awareness one step at a time. For example, try to focus your listening on what others are saying to you about you. What can you learn about yourself that might be useful? Then try the other strategies.

Strategies for

Self-Disclosing

One of the most important forms of communication that you can engage in is talking about yourself, or self-disclosure. Self-disclosure refers to the communication of information about yourself that you normally keep hidden. It may involve information about your values, beliefs, and desires ("I believe in reincarnation"); your behavior ("I shoplifted but was never caught"); or your self-qualities or characteristics ("I'm dyslexic"). Overt and carefully planned statements about yourself as well as slips of the tongue would be all be self-disclosing communications. Similarly, you could self-disclose nonverbally by, for example, wearing gang colors, a wedding ring, a shirt with slogans that reveal your political or social concerns, such as "Pro-Choice" or "Go Green," or posting photos on Facebook. Self-disclosure also may involve your reactions to the feelings of others; for example, when you tell your friend that you're sorry she was fired.

Self-disclosure occurs in all forms of communication. It frequently occurs in small group settings, in public speeches, on television talk shows such as *Maury* and *The Jerry Springer Show*, and even on the talk shows of Jay Leno, David Letterman, and Jimmy Kimmel, for example. And self-disclosure can occur not only in face-to-face settings but also online. On social network sites such as Twitter or Facebook, for example, a great deal of self-disclosure goes on, as it does when people reveal themselves in personal e-mails, newsgroups, and blog posts. In fact, reciprocal self-disclosure occurs more quickly and at higher levels online than it does in face-to-face interactions.

The ways in which you self-disclose are influenced by a variety of factors. See the & Box, Factors Influencing Self-Disclosure.

Factors Influencing Self-Disclosure

Many factors influence whether or not you disclose, what you disclose, and to whom you disclose. Among the most important factors are who you are, your culture, your gender, who your listeners are, and what your topic is.

- **Who you are:** Highly sociable and extroverted people self-disclose more than those who are less sociable and more introverted. People who are apprehensive about talking in general also self-disclose less than do those who are more comfortable in communicating. Competent people and those with high self-esteem engage in self-disclosure more than less competent people and those with low self-esteem.
- **Your culture:** Different cultures view self-disclosure differently. People in the United States, for example, disclose more than do those in Great Britain, Germany, Japan, or Puerto Rico. Americans also reported greater self-disclosure when communicating with other Americans than when communicating interculturally. In Japan it's considered undesirable for colleagues to reveal personal information, whereas in much of the United States it's expected.

- **Your gender:** Women disclose more than men about their previous romantic relationships, their feelings about their closest same-sex friends, their greatest fears, and what they don't like about their partners. A notable exception occurs in initial encounters. Here men will disclose more intimately than women, perhaps "in order to control the relationship's development".
- **Your listeners:** Because you disclose on the basis of the support you receive, you disclose to people you like and to people you trust and love. You also come to like those to whom you disclose. Not surprisingly, you're more likely to disclose to people who are close to you in age. Social network sites enable you to regulate who will have access to your messages. For example, Twitter enables you to keep your tweets private (open only to those who follow you) or to allow anyone, even those without a Twitter account, to read your tweets.
- **Your topic:** You're more likely to self-disclose about some topics than others; for example, you're more likely to disclose information about your job or hobbies than about your sex life or financial situation. You're also more likely to disclose favorable than unfavorable information. Generally, the more personal and negative the topic, the less likely you'll be to self-disclose.

Self-disclosure has both significant rewards and dangers. In making choices about whether or not to disclose, consider both. Among the rewards of self-disclosure is that it helps you gain greater self-knowledge: a new perspective on yourself, a deeper understanding of your own behavior. Through self-disclosure you may bring to consciousness a great deal that you might otherwise keep from conscious analysis. Because you understand the messages of another person largely to the extent that you understand the person, self-disclosure is an essential condition for communication and relationship effectiveness. Self-disclosure helps you achieve a closer relationship with the person to whom you self-disclose and increases relationship satisfaction.

Within a sexual relationship, self-disclosure increases sexual rewards and general relationship satisfaction; after all, it's largely through self-disclosure that you learn what another person likes and dislikes. Self-disclosure also seems to have a positive effect on physiological health. People who self-disclose are less vulnerable to illnesses. Not surprisingly, health benefits also result from disclosing in e-mails. For example, bereavement over the death of someone very close is linked to physical illness for those who bear this alone and in silence. But it's unrelated to any physical problems for those who share their grief with others.

There are also considerable potential personal, relational, and professional risks to self-disclosure. If you self-disclose aspects of your life that vary greatly from the values of those to whom you disclose, you incur personal risks; you may experience rejection from even your closest friends and family members. Even in close and long-lasting relationships, self-disclosure can pose relational risks. Total self-disclosure may prove threatening to a relationship by causing a decrease in mutual attraction, trust, or any of the bonds holding the individuals together. Revealing political views or attitudes toward different religious or racial groups may open you to professional risks and create problems on the job, as may disclosing any health problems, such as being HIV positive. Teachers, for example, who disclose former or current drug use or cohabitation with students may find themselves denied tenure, teaching at undesirable hours, arrested, and/or a victim of "budget cuts."

In making your choice between disclosing and not disclosing, keep in mind—in addition to the advantages and dangers already noted—the irreversible nature of communication. Regardless of how many times you may try to qualify something or take it back, once you have disclosed, you cannot un-disclose. Nor can you erase the conclusions and inferences listeners have made on the basis of your disclosures.

Because of the considerable rewards and dangers of self-disclosure, consider carefully the following factors. These strategies will help you raise the right questions before you make what must be your decision.

- **Consider the motivation for the self-disclosure.** Self-disclosure should be motivated by a concern for the relationship, for the others involved, and for yourself.

- **Consider the appropriateness of the self-disclosure.** Self-disclosure should be appropriate to the context and to the relationship between you and your listener. Before making any significant self-disclosure, ask whether this is the right time (Do you both have the time to discuss this in the length it requires?) and place (Is the place private enough?). Ask, too, whether this self-disclosure is appropriate to the relationship. Generally, the more intimate the disclosure, the closer the relationship should be.

- **Consider the disclosures of the other person.** During your disclosures, give the other person a chance to reciprocate with his or her own disclosures. If the other person does not reciprocate, reassess your own self-disclosures. It may be that for this person at this time and in this context, your disclosures are not welcome or appropriate.

- **Consider the possible burdens self-disclosure might entail.** Carefully weigh the potential problems that you may incur as a result of your disclosure. Can you afford to lose your job if you disclose your prison record? Are you willing to risk relational difficulties if you disclose your infidelities (on the *The Jerry Springer Show,* for example)? Also, ask yourself whether you're placing burdens on the listener. For example, consider the person who swears his or her mother-in-law to secrecy and then discloses having an affair with a neighbor. This disclosure clearly places an unfair burden on the mother-in-law.

Try It

Consider your own self-disclosures by focusing on one thing you've considered revealing to another person. Review the rewards and dangers of disclosing this specific information to this specific person. Analyze the potential consequences as objectives and as logically as you can. Then make your decision.

Strategies for

Self-Disclosing: Facilitation and Responding

When someone discloses to you, it's usually a sign of trust and affection. In carrying out this most important receiver function, consider the following strategies:

- **Practice the skills of effective and active listening.** Listen actively, listen politely, listen for different levels of meaning, listen with empathy, and listen with an open mind. Express an understanding of the speaker's feelings in order to give the speaker the opportunity to see his or her feelings more objectively and through the eyes of another. Ask questions to ensure your own understanding and to signal your interest and attention.

- **Support and reinforce the discloser.** Try to refrain from evaluation, concentrating on understanding and empathizing. Make your supportiveness clear to the discloser through your verbal and nonverbal responses; for example, maintain eye contact, lean toward the speaker, ask relevant questions, and echo the speaker's thoughts and feelings.

- **Be willing to reciprocate.** Your own disclosures (made in response to the other person's disclosures), demonstrate your understanding of the other's meanings and your willingness to communicate on a meaningful level.

The Dyadic Effect

In American culture we're more likely to disclose when the person we're with discloses. This dyadic effect (what one person does, the other person does likewise) probably leads us to feel more secure and reinforces our own self-disclosing behavior. Disclosures are also more intimate when they're made in response to the disclosures of others. This dyadic effect is not universal across all cultures, however. For example, although Americans are likely to follow the dyadic effect and reciprocate with explicit, verbal self-disclosure, Koreans aren't. As you can appreciate, this can easily cause intercultural differences; for example, Americans might be insulted if their Korean counterpart didn't reciprocate with self-disclosures that were similar in depth.

- **Keep the disclosures confidential.** If you reveal disclosures to others, negative effects are inevitable. It's interesting to note that one of the netiquette rules of e-mail is that you shouldn't forward mail to third parties without the writer's permission. This rule is useful for self-disclosure generally: Maintain confidentiality; don't pass on disclosures made to you to others without the person's permission.

- **Don't use the disclosures against the person.** Many self-disclosures expose vulnerability or weakness. If you later turn around and use a disclosure against the person, you betray the confidence and trust invested in you. Regardless of how angry you may get, resist the temptation to use the disclosures of others as weapons.

Try It

Reflect on a situation in which someone disclosed something personal to you. How did you react, for example, did you listen actively? Did you support the discloser? Did you reciprocate with disclosures of your own? Did you keep the disclosure confidential? Did you use the disclosures against the person? Keep these strategies in mind for the next time someone discloses to you.

Strategies for

Self-Disclosure: Resisting

Self-disclosure is important in relationships of all kinds—close interpersonal relationships as well as workplace colleague relationships. If you're going to get to know someone, there has to be some significant self-disclosure. And yet, there are times—many times—when you're pressured to self-disclose by a friend, colleague, or romantic partner, for example, but for one reason or another, you may not be ready. In this event, consider these strategies:

- **Don't be pushed.** Although there may be certain legal or ethical reasons for disclosing, generally, if you don't want to disclose, you don't have to. Don't be pushed into disclosing because others are doing it or because you're asked to.

- **Delay a decision.** If you don't want to say no directly, but still don't want to disclose, delay the decision. Say something like "That's pretty personal; let me think about that before I make a fool of myself" or "This isn't really a good time (or place) to talk about this; I'll get back to you and we'll talk."

- **Be indirect and move to another topic.** Avoid the question and change the subject. This is a polite way of saying, "I'm not talking about it," and may be the preferred choice in certain situations. Most often people will get the hint and understand your refusal to disclose.

- **Be assertive in your refusal to disclose.** Say, very directly, "I'd rather not talk about that now" or "Now is not the time for this type of discussion." More specific strategies for communicating assertiveness are offered in the chapter on Assertiveness.

Try It

The next time you're pressured to self-disclose try one or more of these strategies. And then, in a less pressured moment, reflect on your decision to resist disclosing and the strategies you used. Can you improve your strategic avoidance?

Strategies for

Self-Esteem

Self-esteem is a measure of how valuable you think you are; people with high self-esteem think very highly of themselves, whereas people with low self-esteem view themselves negatively. The basic idea behind building self-esteem is that when you feel good about yourself—about who you are and what you're capable of doing—you'll perform better. When you think like a success, you're more likely to act like a success. Conversely, when you think you're a failure, you're more likely to act like a failure.

When you get up to give a speech and you visualize yourself being successful and effective, you're more likely to give a good speech. Increasing self-esteem will, therefore, help you to function more effectively in school, in personal and social relationships, and in careers. Before reading about ways to increase self-esteem, consider your own self-esteem by asking yourself if each of the following is true or false about you:

1. Generally, I feel I have to be successful in all things.
2. Several of my acquaintances are often critical or negative of what I do and how I think.
3. I often tackle projects that I know are impossible to complete to my satisfaction.
4. When I focus on the past, I focus more often on my failures than on my successes and on my negative rather than my positive qualities.
5. I make little effort to improve my personal and social skills.

"True" responses to the questions suggest ways of thinking that can get in the way of building positive self-esteem. "False" responses would indicate that you are thinking much like a self-esteem coach would want you to think.

Here are some ways you can increase your self-esteem:

- **Attack your self-destructive beliefs.** Challenge beliefs you have about yourself that are unproductive or that make it more difficult for you to achieve your goals. Self-destructive beliefs set unrealistically high standards and therefore almost always lead to failure. As a result, you may develop a negative self-image, seeing yourself as someone who constantly fails. So replace these self-destructive beliefs with more productive ones, such as "I succeed in many things, but I don't have to succeed in everything" and "It would be nice to be loved by everyone, but it isn't necessary to my happiness." For some of the major self-destructive beliefs see the & Box, Self-Destructive Beliefs.

Self-Destructive Beliefs

Here, for example, are some beliefs that are likely to prove self-destructive and parallel the five statements presented earlier.

- The belief that you have **to be perfect**; this causes you to try to perform at unrealistically high levels at work, school, and home; anything short of perfection is unacceptable.
- The belief that you **have to be strong**, which tells you that weakness and any of the more vulnerable emotions—like sadness, compassion, or loneliness—are wrong.

- The belief that you have **to please others** and that your worthiness depends on what others think of you.
- The belief that you have **to hurry up**; this compels you to do things quickly, to try to do more than can be reasonably expected in any given amount of time.
- The belief that you have **to take on more responsibilities** than any one person can be expected to handle.

- **Seek out nourishing people.** Psychologist Carl Rogers drew a distinction between *noxious* and *nourishing* people. Noxious people criticize and find fault with just about everything. Nourishing people, on the other hand, are positive and optimistic. Most important, nourishing people reward us, they stroke us, they make us feel good about ourselves. To enhance your self-esteem, seek out these people—and avoid noxious people, those who make you feel negatively about yourself. At the same time, seek to become more nourishing yourself so that you each build up the other's self-esteem.

- **Work on projects that will result in success.** Some people want to fail (or so it seems). Often, they select projects that will result in failure simply because these projects are impossible to complete. Avoid this trap; select projects that will result in success. Each success will help build self-esteem, and each success will make the next success a little easier. If a project does fail, recognize that this does not mean that *you're* a failure. Everyone fails somewhere along the line. Failure is something that happens; it's not necessarily something you've created. It's not something inside you. Further, your failing once does not mean that you will fail the next time. So learn to put failure in perspective.

- **Remind yourself of your successes.** Some people have a tendency to focus, sometimes too much, on their failures, their missed opportunities, their social mistakes. If your objective is to correct what you did wrong or to identify the skills that you need to correct these failures, then focusing on failures can have some positive value. But if you focus on failure without thinking about plans for correction, then you're probably just making life more difficult for yourself and limiting your self-esteem. To counteract the tendency to recall failures, remind yourself of your successes. Recall these successes both intellectually and emotionally. Realize why they were successes, and relive the emotional experience—the feelings you had when you sank that winning basketball or aced that test or helped that friend overcome a personal problem.

- **Secure affirmation.** Affirmations are statements asserting that something is true. In discussions of self-concept and self-awareness, the word *affirmation* is used to refer to positive statements about you, statements asserting that something good or positive is true of you. It's frequently recommended that you remind yourself of your successes with self-affirmations—that you focus on your good deeds; on your positive qualities, strengths, and virtues; on your productive and meaningful relationships with friends, loved ones, and relatives.

  Self-affirmations include statements such as "I'm a worthy person," "I'm responsible and can be depended upon," and "I'm capable of loving and being loved." The idea behind this advice is that the way you talk to yourself will influence what you think of yourself. If you *affirm* yourself—if you tell yourself that you're a success, that others like you, that you will succeed on the next test, and that you will be welcomed when asking for a date—you will soon come to feel more positive about yourself.

Some researchers, however, argue that self-affirmations—although extremely popular in self-help books—may not be very helpful. These critics contend that if you have low self-esteem, you're not going to believe your self-affirmations, because you don't have a high opinion of yourself to begin with. They propose that the alternative to self-affirmation is to secure affirmation from others. You'd do this by, for example, becoming more competent in communication and interacting with more positive people. In this way, you'd get more positive feedback from others—which, these researchers argue, is more helpful than self-talk in raising self-esteem.

Try It

Try one of the strategies suggested here for a day or two. For example, try to identify one or two self-destructive beliefs that you have and consciously consider reasons why these beliefs are self-destructive and why you'd be better off (and think more highly of yourself) if you got rid of them.

Strategies for

Small Talk

Small talk is pervasive; all of us engage in small talk. Sometimes, we use small talk as a preface to big talk. For example, before a conference with your boss or even an employment interview, you're likely to engage in some preliminary small talk. *How you doing? I'm pleased this weather has finally cleared up. That's a great looking jacket.* The purpose here is to ease into the major topic or the big talk. Take a look at the & Box, How Do You Small Talk?, to get an idea of how you behave in small-talk situations.

&

How Do You Small Talk?

Respond to each of these questions in terms of your normal ways of behaving. Avoid trying to give "correct" responses.

_____ 1. On an elevator with three or four strangers, I'd be most likely to
  a. seek to avoid interacting.
  b. respond to another but not initiate interaction.
  c. be the first to talk.

_____ 2. When I'm talking with someone and I meet a friend who doesn't know the person I'm with, I'd be most apt to
  a. avoid introducing them.

b. wait until they introduce each other.
c. introduce them to each other.

_____ 3. At a party with people I've never met before, I'd be most likely to
a. wait for someone to talk to me.
b. nonverbally indicate that you're receptive to someone interacting with you.
c. initiate interaction with others nonverbally and verbally.

_____ 4. When confronted with someone who doesn't want to end the conversation, I'd be most apt to
a. just stick it out and listen.
b. tune out the person and hope time goes by quickly.
c. end it firmly myself.

_____ 5. When the other person monologues, I'd be most apt to
a. listen politely.
b. try to change the focus.
c. exit as quickly as possible.

The ***a*** responses are unassertive, the ***b*** responses are indirect (not totally unassertive but not assertive either), and the ***c*** responses are direct and assertive. Very likely, if you answered with 4 or 5 ***c*** responses, you're comfortable and satisfied with your small talk experiences. Lots of ***a*** responses would indicate some level of dissatisfaction and discomfort with the experience of small talk. If you had lots of ***b*** responses then you probably experience both satisfaction and dissatisfaction with small talk.

Sometimes, small talk is a politeness strategy and a bit more extensive way of saying hello as you pass someone in the hallway or a neighbor you meet at the post office. And, so you might say, *Good seeing you, Jack. You're ready for the big meeting?* or, *"See you in cafeteria at 1."*

Sometimes, your relationship with another person revolves totally around small talk, perhaps with your barber or hair dresser, a colleague at work, your next door neighbor, or a student you sit next to in class. In these relationships neither person makes an effort to deepen the relationship and it remains on a small talk level.

Although "small," this talk still requires the application of the communication skills for "big" talk. Here are a few strategies for more effective small talk.

- **Talk about the non-controversial.** Topics of small talk must not be something that you and the other person are likely to disagree on. If a topic is likely to arouse deep emotions or different points of view, then it is probably not a small talk topic.

- **Talk little.** Small talk is usually short in duration, a factor that helps make this talk non-controversial. Because of the context in which small talk occurs—waiting on line to get into a movie or for a store to open—it allows for only a brief interaction.

- **Be positive.** No one likes a negative doom-sayer.

- **Be sensitive to leave-taking cues.** Small talk is necessarily brief, but at times one person may want it to be a preliminary to the big talk and another person may see it as the sum of the interaction.

- **Stress similarities rather than differences.** This is a good way to ensure that this small talk is non-controversial.

- **Answer questions with some elaboration.** This will give the other person information that can then be used to interact with you. Let's say someone sees a book you're carrying and says, "I see you're taking communication." If you say, simply "yes," you've not given the other person anything to talk with you about. Instead, if you say, "Yes, it's a great course; I think I'm going to major in communication" then you have given the other person information that can be addressed. The more elaborate answer also signals your willingness to engage in small talk. Of course, if you do not want to interact, then a simple one-word response will help you achieve your goal.

Try It

The next time you're on an elevator or on line at the bank or supermarket, try some of the strategies for small talk suggested here. How would you describe the interaction? What could have been improved?

Strategies for

Violence Management

Violence is a sad fact of many relationships. The violence can take a variety of forms. Verbal or emotional abuse may include humiliating you; engaging in economic abuse such as controlling the finances or preventing you from working; and/or isolating, criticizing, or stalking you. Not surprisingly, people who use verbal or emotional abuse are more likely than others to escalate to physical abuse. Physical abuse includes threats of violence as well as pushing, hitting, slapping, kicking, choking, throwing things at you, and breaking things. Sexual abuse involves touching that is unwanted, accusations of sexual infidelity without reason, forced sex, and references to you in abusive sexual terms. Some of the warning signs are identified in the & Box, Warning Signs of Violence.

&

Warning Signs of Violence

It's obviously of great help to be able to identify the warning signs of relationship violence. Here, for example, are a few signs compiled by the State University of New York at Buffalo; you might want to use this list to start thinking about your own relationship or those that you know of (http://ubcounseling.buffalo,edu/warnings/shtml). It may be a warning sign if your partner:

- belittles, insults, or ignores you
- controls pieces of your life; for example, the way you dress or who you can be friends with
- gets jealous without reason
- can't handle sexual frustration without anger
- is so angry or threatening that you've changed your life so as not to provoke additional anger

Whether you're a victim or a perpetrator of relationship violence, it is important to seek professional help (and, of course, the help of friends and family where appropriate). If your partner has been violent:

- **Realize that you're not alone.** There are other people who suffer similarly, and there is a mechanism in place to help you.

- **Realize you're not at fault.** You did not deserve to be the victim of violence.

- **Plan for your safety.** Violence, if it occurred once, is likely to occur again, and part of your thinking needs to be devoted to your own safety.

- **Know your resources**—the phone numbers you need to contact help, the locations of money and a spare set of keys.

If you are the violent partner:

- **Realize that you too are not alone.** You too are a victim and in need of help and support.

- **Know that you can change.** It won't necessarily be easy or quick, but you can change.

- **Own your own behaviors.** Take responsibility. This is an essential step if any change is to occur.

- **Seek professional help.** This is crucial; if you are prone to violent behavior you need to discover how you can manage it.

Try It

Reflect on your own relationships and those relationships you know about. Is violence a part of the relationship? If so, then you need to do something about it.

Strategies for

Workplace Communication

The organization in today's world is largely a communication network and how messages move around in the organization is crucial to its success and survival. Although each type of workplace communication requires somewhat specialized rules and forms, here are a few general communication strategies:

- **Be respectful of a colleague's time.** This guideline suggests lots of specifics; for example, don't copy those who don't need to be copied, be brief and organized, respond to requests as soon as possible and when not possible, alert the other person that, for example, "the figures will be sent as soon as they arrive, probably by the end of the day." Most important, perhaps, is to be clear. For example, recognize that your own specialty has a technical jargon that others outside your specialty might not know. Clarify when and as needed.

- **Be respectful of a person's territory.** Humans, like animals, are very territorial. This is especially true in the business world where status distinctions are very important and govern the rules of territoriality. So, for example, don't invade another's office or desk space (personally or even with the scent you wear) and don't overspend your welcome. In brief, treat another's work space as someone's private territory into which you must be invited.

- **Follow the rules for effective electronic communication.** These rules will differ from one workplace to another so look within your specific organization for rules governing the use of e-mails, Internet game playing, cell phones, social networking, and instant messaging.

- **Discard your Facebook and texting grammar and spelling**. These may be seen as not showing sufficient respect for someone high in the company hierarchy. The general suggestion offered for people writing into newsgroups is appropriate here as well; watch how other people write before writing yourself. If you find no guidance here, your best bet is to write as if your email is being graded by your English professor. This means editing for conciseness, proof reading, and spell and grammar checking.

- **Use the appropriate medium for sending messages.** Generally, the rule is to respond in kind—for example, if a question is asked in email, answer it in email.

- **Avoid touching except in shaking hands.** Touching is often interpreted as a sexual overture, so it's best avoided on the job. Touching may also imply a familiarity that the other person may not welcome. Your best bet is to avoid initiating touching but don't be offended if others put their arm on our shoulder or pat you on the back. In some cases, a slight touch on the hand or shoulder is appropriate and welcomed.

- **Be willing to communicate.** Be open to hearing other's comments. Be willing to listen to these messages even when they're critical and demonstrate that willingness with appropriate eye contact, posture, and feedback cues. At the same time, when you're offering negative comments be sure to do so privately so as not to damage the image of those singled out. Allow the person to save face.

- **Understand the variety of purposes the grapevine serves.** Its speed and general accuracy make it an ideal medium to carry many of the social communications that effectively bind workers together. So listen carefully; it will give you an insider's view of the organization and will help you understand those with whom you work. But, treat grapevine information as tentative, as possibly but not necessarily true. Although grapevine information is generally accurate, it's often incomplete and ambiguous; it may also contain crucial distortions.

- **Be mindful of all your organizational communications.** The potentially offensive joke that you e-mail a colleague can easily be forwarded to the very people who may take offense.

- **Treat everyone politely.** Treat even the newest intern with politeness—as if that person will one day be your boss. He or she may well be. For more on this see the *Politeness in Conversation* and *Politeness Online* chapters.

Try It

Try first to observe the rules for communicating within your workplace, using the strategies noted here as a guide for what to look for. Then ask yourself how you can communicate more appropriately within this specific workplace.

In a Nutshell: A Summary of 50 Essential Communication Strategies

Here in the proverbial nutshell are the strategies for easy review and to use as quick memory joggers.

Advice Giving and Receiving

Giving Advice

- Listen
- Empathize
- Be tentative.
- Ensure understanding.
- Keep the interaction confidential.
- Avoid *should* statements.

Responding to Advice

- Accept the advice
- Avoid negative responses.
- Interact with the advice.
- Express appreciation.

Anger Management

- Get ready to communicate calmly and logically.
- Examine your communication choices.

- Consider the advantages of delaying the expression of anger.
- Remember that different cultures have different display rules
- Apply the relevant skills of communication.
- Recall the irreversibility of communication.

Apologizing

- Admit wrongdoing
- Be apologetic.
- Be specific.
- Empathize.
- Give assurance that this will not happen again.
- Avoid excuses.
- Choose the appropriate channel.

Apprehension

- Reduce the newness of the communication situation by gaining experience
- Reduce your self-focus by visualizing public speaking as conversation
- Reduce your perceived differentness from the audience by stressing similarity
- Reduce your fear of failure by thoroughly preparing and practicing
- Reduce your anxiety by moving about and breathing deeply
- Avoid chemicals as tension relievers

Argumentativeness

- Treat disagreements as objectively as possible.
- Avoid attacking the other person.
- Reaffirm the other person's sense of competence.
- Avoid interrupting.
- Stress equality.

- Express interest in the other person.
- Avoid presenting your arguments too emotionally.
- Allow the other person to save face.

Assertiveness

- Analyze Assertive Communications.
- Rehearse Assertive Communications
- Communicate Assertively.

Attractiveness

- Express similarities.
- Keep in touch.
- Stress the positive.
- Be liking.
- Reinforce.
- Gesture
- Nod and lean forward
- Smile
- Make eye contact in moderation
- Touch in moderation when appropriate.
- Use vocal variation.
- Use silence.
- Establish physical closeness.
- Present a pleasant smell.
- Dress appropriately to the situation.

Complimenting

- Be real and honest.
- Compliment in moderation.
- Be totally complimentary.
- Be specific.
- Be personal in your own feelings.

Conflict Management

- Set the stage.

- Define the conflict.
- Examine possible solutions.
- Test the solution.
- Evaluate the solution.
- Accept or reject the solution.
- Wrap it up.

Conversational Closings

- Reflect back on the conversation.
- Be direct.
- Refer to future interaction.
- Ask for closure.
- Express your enjoyment of the interaction.

Conversation Openings

- Use self-references.
- Refer to the other person.
- Refer to the relationship.
- Make reference to the context.

Conversational Cooperation

- Follow the maxim of quantity
- Follow the maxim of quality
- Follow the maxim of relation
- Follow the maxim of manner

Critical Thinking

- Extensionalize
- Avoid allness
- Avoid fact-Inference
- Avoid indiscrimination
- Avoid polarization.
- Avoid static evaluation

Criticizing

- Own your thoughts and feelings.
- Be clear.
- Avoid ordering or directing
- Consider the context of the criticism.

Dialogue

- Avoid requesting self-approval statements.
- Keep the channels of communication open.
- Paraphrase or summarize what the other person has said
- Request clarification as necessary.
- Avoid negative criticism and negative personal judgments.

Disclaiming

- Hedge.
- Credential yourself
- Ask for a sin license.
- Establish your cognitive abilities.
- Appeal for the suspension of judgment.

Emotional Expression

- Be specific.
- Describe the reasons you're feeling as you are.
- Address mixed feelings.
- Anchor your emotions in the present.
- Own your feelings; take personal responsibility for your feelings.
- Ask for what you want.
- Respect emotional boundaries.

Emotional Responding

- Look at nonverbal cues to understand the individual's feelings.

- Look for cues as to what the person wants you to do.
- Use active listening techniques.
- Empathize.
- Focus on the other person.
- Remember the irreversibility of communication.

Empathy

- Be clear.
- Focus
- Reflect
- Disclose
- Address mixed messages
- Acknowledge importance.

Expressiveness

- Use vocal variation.
- Use appropriate gestures.
- Give feedback.
- Smile.
- Communicate expressiveness in ways that are culturally sensitive.

Feedback

- Focus on the behavior or the message.
- Begin with the positive.
- Ask for feedback on your feedback
- Give feedback calmly.

Feedforward

- Use feedforward to estimate the receptivity of the person to what you're going to say.
- Use feedforward that's consistent with your subsequent message.

- The more important or complex the message, the more important and more extensive your feedforward needs to be.
- Use feedforward to cushion shocking messages.

Flexibility

- Appreciate your options.
- Contextualize
- Recognize constant change.
- Focus on differences.

Flirting

- Maintain an open posture;
- Make eye contact
- Smile
- Touch the person's hand
- Mirror the other's behaviors.
- Introduce yourself.
- Ask a question
- Compliment
- Be polite

Friendship Development

- Serve a utility function.
- Engage in affirmation.
- Be ego supportive.
- Be stimulating.
- Provide security.

Grief-Stricken and Communication

- Confirm the other person and the person's emotions.
- Give the person permission to grieve.
- Avoid trying to focus on the bright side.

- Encourage the person to express feelings and talk about the loss.
- Be especially sensitive to leave-taking cues.
- Let the person know you care and are available.

Heterosexist Talk

- Avoid offensive mannerisms
- Avoid "complimenting" gay men and lesbians by saying that they "don't look it".
- Avoid making the assumption that every gay or lesbian knows what every other gay or lesbian is thinking.
- Avoid relying on stereotypes.
- Avoid overattribution.
- Remember that relationship milestones are important to all people
- Use appropriate cultural identifiers

Immediacy

- Self-disclose.
- Refer to the other person's good qualities.
- Express a positive view.
- Talk about commonalities.
- Demonstrate responsiveness
- Express psychological closeness and openness.
- Maintain appropriate eye contact.
- Smile.
- Focus on the other person's remarks.
- Express positiveness through your facial expressions.
- Express immediacy with an awareness of personality differences.
- Express immediacy with cultural sensitivity.
- Secure feedback on your immediacy efforts.

Introductions

- Admit it when you forget the person's name.
- Don't be forced to self-disclose.
- Be culturally sensitive.
- Observe rank and gender differences.

Listening

In receiving:

- Focus your attention
- Avoid distractions
- Maintain your role as listener

In understanding

- Avoid assuming you understand
- See the speaker's messages from the speaker's point of view.
- Ask questions
- Rephrase (paraphrase)

In remembering

- Focus
- Organize
- Unite
- Repeat

In evaluating

- Resist evaluation
- Distinguish facts from opinions
- Identify any biases
- Recognize fallacious forms of "reasoning

In responding

- Support the speaker
- Own your responses
- Resist "responding to another's feelings" with "solving the person's problems"
- Focus on the other person.
- Avoid being a thought-completing listener

Listening Actively

- Paraphrase the speaker's meaning.
- Express understanding of the speaker's feelings.
- Ask questions.

Lying Detection

- Look for evidence that the person is holding back.
- Look for leaks.
- Look for illogical connections.
- Look for uncooperative behavior.
- Look at body tension
- Look at pupil dilation
- Look for variations in pitch.
- Look for errors and hesitations
- Look at hand and leg movements
- Look for self-touching movements

Metacommunicating

- Explain your feelings.
- Give clear feedforward.
- Paraphrase.
- Ask for clarification.
- Use metacommunication to talk about your talk.

Mindfulness

- Create and recreate categories.
- Be open to new information and points of view.
- Beware of relying too heavily on first impressions.
- Consider the Possibility of Misinterpretation.
- Focus on the Uniqueness of the Situation.
- Pause and Think.

Perceptual Accuracy

- Analyze Impressions.
- Check Perceptions.

- Reduce Uncertainty
- Increase Cultural Sensitivity.

Politeness in Conversation

- Follow the maxim of tact
- Follow the maxim of generosity
- Follow the maxim of approbation
- Follow the maxim of modesty
- Follow the maxim of agreement
- Follow the maxim of sympathy

Politeness Online

- Familiarize yourself with the site before contributing.
- Be brief.
- Be gentle.
- Don't shout.
- Be discrete.
- Don't spam or flame.
- Avoid offensive language.
- Be considerate.
- Don't advertise.
- Don't plagiarize.
- Don't brag.

Power

- Respond to the eyebrow flash.
- Avoid adaptors.
- Use consistent packaging.
- Select the right chairs.
- Shake
- Dress conservatively.
- Use facial expressions and gestures as appropriate.
- Walk slowly and deliberately.
- Maintain eye contact.

- Avoid vocalized pauses.
- Maintain reasonably close distances between yourself and those with whom you interact.
- Relax
- Vary your speech rate, volume, and pitch as appropriate to the conversation.
- Accommodate
- Move and gesture purposefully.
- Take up your space.
- Still your feet.
- Avoid hesitations.
- Avoid too many intensifiers.
- Avoid disqualifiers.
- Avoid tag questions.
- Avoid self-critical statements.
- Avoid slang and vulgar expressions.

Relationship Development

- Be nice.
- Communicate
- Be open
- Give assurances.
- Share joint activities.
- Be positive
- Focus on improving yourself
- Be empathic.

Relationship Deterioration

- Withdraw.
- Reduce self-disclosure.
- Deceive.
- Decrease positive and increase negative messages.

Relationship Dissolution

- Break the loneliness-depression cycle.
- Take time out.
- Bolster your self-esteem.
- Remove or avoid uncomfortable relationship symbols.
- Become mindful of your own relationship patterns.

Relationship Repair

- Recognize the problem
- Engage in Productive Communication and Conflict Resolution
- Pose Possible Solutions
- Affirm each other
- Integrate solutions into normal behavior
- Risk

Self-Awareness

- Listen to others
- Increase your open self
- Seek information about yourself
- Dialogue with yourself

Self-Disclosing

- Consider the motivation for the self-disclosure.
- Consider the appropriateness of the self-disclosure.
- Consider the disclosures of the other person.
- Consider the possible burdens self-disclosure might entail.

Self-Disclosing: Facilitating and Responding

- Practice the skills of effective and active listening.
- Support and reinforce the discloser.

- Be willing to reciprocate.
- Keep the disclosures confidential.
- Don't use the disclosures against the person.

Self-Disclosing: Resisting

- Don't be pushed.
- Delay a decision.
- Be indirect and move to another topic.
- Be assertive in your refusal to disclose

Self-Esteem

- Attack your self-destructive beliefs
- Seek out nourishing people
- Work on projects that will result in success
- Remind yourself of your successes
- Secure affirmation

Small Talk

- Be positive.
- Answer questions with some elaboration.
- Stress similarities rather than differences.
- Be sensitive to leave-taking cues.

Violence Management

- Realize that you're not alone.
- Realize you're not at fault.
- Plan for your safety.
- Know your resources
- Know that you can change.
- Own your own behaviors.

Workplace Communication

- Be respectful of a colleague's time.
- Be respectful of a person's territory.

- Follow the rules for effective electronic communication.
- Discard your Facebook grammar and spelling.
- Use the appropriate medium for sending messages.
- Avoid touching except in shaking hands.
- Be willing to communicate.
- Understand the variety of purposes the grapevine serves.
- Be mindful of all your organizational communications.
- Treat everyone politely.

References

Welcome

References to politeness are given below under the entry for Politeness in Conversation and Politeness Online. The steps of reflective thinking are the work of educational theorist John Dewey, *How We Think* (Boston: Heath, 1910). For the study on married couples conflicts see: Schutz, A. (1999). It was your fault! Self-serving biases in autobiographical accounts of conflicts in married couples. *Journal of Social and Personal Relationships* 16, 193–208. Many of the principles owe their formulation to the work of Paul Watzlawick and his associates. See, for example, P. Watzlawick, J. H. Beavin, & D. D. Jackson, *Pragmatics of human communication: A study of interactional patterns, pathologies, and paradoxes* (New York, NY: Norton, 1976); P. Watzlawick, *The language of change: Elements of therapeutic communication* (New York: Basic Books, 1978), and P. Watzlawick, *How real is real? Confusion, disinformation, communication: An anecdotal introduction to communications theory* (New York: Vintage, 1977).

1. Advice Giving and Receiving

The best sources on giving and receiving advice are the many and varied websites—just search for *advice* with your favorite search engine.

2. Anger Management

SCREAM and anger management are discussed in more detail in J. A. DeVito, SCREAM before you scream. *Etc: A Review of General Semantics* 60 (spring, 2003), 42–45. On the arguments for and against expressing anger see C. Tavris, *Anger: The misunderstood emotion*, 2nd ed. (New York: Simon & Schuster, 1989) and U. Hess, A. Kappas, G. J. McHugo, J. T. Lanzetta, et al., The facilitative effect of facial expression on the self-generation of emotion. *International Journal of Psychophysiology*, 12 (May, 1992), 251–265.

3. Apologizing

Among the better websites dealing with apologizing is the Harvard Business School Working Knowledge website.

4. Apprehension

The research on communication apprehension is enormous but the best single source in which original research is summarized and practical recommendations are offered—and on which I drew extensively—is V. P. Richmond, & J. C. McCroskey, *Communication: Apprehension, avoidance, and effectiveness* (5th ed.). Boston: Allyn & Bacon, 1998). The factors that create apprehension are from M. J. Beatty, Situational and predispositional correlates of public speaking anxiety. *Communication Education, 37* (1988), 28–39. For cognitive restructuring see A. Ellis, *How to stubbornly refuse to make yourself miserable about anything, yes anything* (Secaucus, NJ: Lyle Stuart, 1988). For systematic desensitization see J. Wolpe, *Psychotherapy by reciprocal inhibition.* Stanford, CA: Stanford University Press, 1957). For performance visualization see J. Ayres, Performance visualization and behavioral disruption: A clarification. *Communication Reports, 18* (2005), 55–63.

5. Argumentativeness

Argumentativeness was first presented in D. A. Infante, & A. S. Rancer, A conceptualization and measure of argumentativeness. *Journal of Personality Assessment* 46 (1982), 72–80. A more recent treatment of the research, theory, and practical applications may be found in A. S. Rancer, & T. A. Avtgis, *Argumentative and aggressive communication: Theory, research, and application* (Thousand Oaks, CA: Sage, 2006).

6. Assertiveness

On the relationship of assertiveness to hopelessness see D. M. Velting, Personality and negative expectations: Trait structure of the Beck Hopelessness Scale. *Personality and Individual Differences* 26 (1999), 913–921. Cultural differences are discussed in C. A. Thompson, & D. W. Klopf, An analysis of social style among disparate cultures. *Communication Research Reports* 8 (1991), 65–72 and C. A. Thompson, D. W. Klopf, & S. Ishii, A comparison of social style between Japanese and Americans. *Communication Research Reports* 8 (1991), 165–172. A useful guide to assertiveness is S. A. Bower, & G. H. Bower, *Asserting yourself: A practical guide for positive change.* Cambridge, MA: DaCapo Press, 2005).

7. Attractiveness

On universal attractiveness see J. F. Brody, Notions of beauty transcend culture, new study suggests. *New York Times* (March 21, 1994), A14. On reciprocity of liking see P. W. Eastwick, & E. J. Finkel, Reciprocity of Liking. In Harry T. Reis & Susan Sprecher (Eds.), *Encyclopedia of human relationships* (pp. 1333-1336). (Thousand Oaks, CA: Sage, 2009).

8. Complimenting

Complimenting is in large part the application of politeness principles—see the references for politeness as well as J. Holmes, Compliments and compliment responses in New Zealand English, *Anthropological Linguistics*, 28 (1986), 485–508 for a cultural perspective.

9. Conflict Management

Conflict and its management continue to command considerable space in the bookstores and online. Among the most useful and that have informed my own thinking are R. R. Blake, R. R., & J. S. Mouton, *The managerial grid III* (3d ed.). Houston, TX: Gulf Publishing, 1984) and J. P. Folger, M. S. Poole, & R. K. Stutman, *Working through conflict: A communication perspective*, 6th ed. (Boston: Allyn & Bacon, 2009).

10. Conversational Closings

11. Conversational Openings

The conversational opening and closing strategies are based on a general model of communication such as that presented in my *Human Communication* (Boston, MA: Pearson, 2012) and *The Interpersonal Communication Book* (Boston, MA: Pearson, 2013). The strategies for closing emails owe much to J. Cohen, An e-mail affliction: The long goodbye. New York Times (May 9, 2002), G6. The types of opening lines comes from C. L. Kleinke, *Meeting and understanding people*. New York, NY: W. H. Freeman, 1986) and C. L. Kleinke, & G. O. Dean, Evaluation of men and women receiving positive and negative responses with various acquaintance strategies. *Journal of Social Behavior and Personality*, 5 (1990), 369–377.

12. Conversational Cooperation

The maxims of cooperation are the work of H. P. Grice, Logic and conversation. In P. Cole & J. L. Morgan (Eds.), *Syntax and semantics*: Vol. 3. Speech acts (pp. 41–58). New York: Seminar Press, 1975). Also see K. Lindblom, Cooperating with Grice: A cross-disciplinary metaperspective on uses of Grice's cooperative principle. *Journal of Pragmatics* 33 (2001), 1601–1623.

13. Critical Thinking

The six thinking hats concept is from E. deBono, E. *The six thinking hats* (New York: Penguin, 1987). All of debono's books are wroth reading; they all offer great insights into critical and creative thinking. Also see my *Brainstorms: How to think more creatively about communication (or about anything else).* (Boston, MA: Pearson, 1996).

14. Criticizing

A useful guide to effective criticism is Mary Lynne Heldmann's *When words hurt: How to keep criticism from undermining your self-esteem* (New York: Ballantine Books, 1988). Research cited includes J. J. Hornsey, M. T. Bath, & S. Gunthorpe, S. "You can criticize because you care": Identity attachment, constructiveness, and the intergroup sensitivity effect. *European Journal of Social Psychology* 34 (September-October, 2004), 499-518 and, on the negative effects of ambiguous criticism, R. Edwards, & R. Bello, Interpretations of messages: The influence of equivocation, face-concerns, and ego-involvement. *Human Communication Research* 27 (2001), 597–631. On microinequities see J. S. Lubin, How to stop the snubs that demoralize you and your colleagues. *Wall Street Journal, Eastern Edition* 244 (December 7, 2004), B1.

15. Dialogue

The concept of dialogue as best articulated by M. Buber, (1958). *I and thou,* 2nd ed. New York: Scribner's. Also see S. McNamee, & K. J. Gergen, eds. *Relational responsibility: Resources for sustainable dialogue* (Thousand Oaks, CA: Sage, 1999).

16. Disclaiming

The five types of disclaimers owe their formulation to J. P. Hewitt, & R. Stokes, Disclaimers. *American Sociological Review* 40 (1975), 1–11. Also see M. L. McLaughlin, *Conversation: How talk is organized* (Thousand Oaks, CA: Sage, 1984).

17. Emotional Expression

18. Emotional Responding

There is much written here. See, for example, G. Goleman, *Emotional intelligence.* New York: Bantam, 1995). For the basic emotions see R. Plutchik, *Emotion: A psycho-evolutionary synthesis* (New York: Harper & Row, 1980); P. Ekman, W. V. Friesen, & P. Ellsworth, *Emotion in the human face: Guidelines for research and an integration of findings* (New York: Pergamon Press, 1972); P. Ekman, *Emotions revealed.* New York: St. Martins, 2003); and D. Matsumoto, M. G. Frank, & H. S. Hwang (Eds.). *Nonverbal communication: Science and applications.* Los Angeles, CA: Sage, 2013). The topic is covered more extensively than here in my *The Interpersonal Communication Book* (Boston, MA: Pearson, 2013).

19. Empathy

See J. Authier, & K. Gustafson, Microtraining: Focusing on specific skills. In E. K. Marshall, P. D. Kurtz, and Associates (Eds.), *Interpersonal helping skills: A guide to training methods, programs, and resources* (pp. 93–130)

(San Francisco: Jossey-Bass, 1982). For the distinction between thinking and feeling empathy see D. Bellafiore, (2005). *Interpersonal conflict and effective communication.* Retrieved from http://www.drbalternatives.com/articles/cc2. html. On gender and empathy see J. Nicolai, & R. Demmel, R. The impact of gender stereotypes on the evaluation of general practitioners' communication skills: An experimental study using transcripts of physical-patient encounters. *Patient Education and Counseling* 69 (December, 2007), 200-205.

20. Expressiveness

On this see B. H. Spitzberg, & W. R. Cupach, *Handbook of interpersonal competence research* (New York: Springer, 1989) and B. H. Spitzberg, & M. L. Hecht, A component model of relational competence. *Human Communication Research,* 10, 1984, 575–599. The cultural material presented here owes most to D. Matsumoto, D. (1991). Cultural influences on facial expressions of emotion. *Southern Communication Journal, 56* (Winter, 1991), 128–137; D. Matsumoto, *People: Psychology from a cultural perspective* (Pacific Grove, CA: Brooks/Cole, 1994); and D. Matsumoto, *Culture and psychology.* (Pacific Grove, CA: Brooks/Cole, 1996).

21. Feedback

22. Feedforward

Both of these concepts are standard Chapter 1 topics in almost any communication textbook but very little research has been conducted on either of them. My own treatments in *The Interpersonal Communication Book* (Boston, MA: Pearson, 2013) and *Human Communication* (Boston, MA: Pearson, 2012) are probably as extensive as any.

23. Flexibility

For research on measuring flexibility see R. P. Hart, R. E. Carlson, & W. F. Eadie, Attitudes toward communication and the assessment of rhetorical sensitivity. *Communication Monographs* 47 (1980), 1–22; M. M. Martin, & C. M. Anderson, (1998). The cognitive flexibility scale: Three validity studies. *Communication Reports* 11 (Winter, 1998), 1–9; and M. M. Martin, & R. B. Rubin, A new measure of cognitive flexibility. *Psychological Reports* 76 (1994), 623–626.

24. Flirting

The suggestions for flirting are based largely on research in nonverbal communication admirably summarized by J. K. Burgoon, L. K. Guerrero, & K. Floyd, (2010). *Nonverbal Communication* (Boston: Allyn & Bacon, 2010) and V. P. Richmond, J. C. McCroskey, & M. L. Hickson, *Nonverbal behavior in interpersonal relations*, 7th ed. (Boston: Allyn & Bacon, 2012).

25. Friendship Development

The friendship needs on which this is based come from research by P. H. Wright, Toward a theory of friendship based on a conception of self. *Human Communication Research* 4 (1978), 196–207 and P. H. Wright, Self-referent motivation and the intrinsic quality of friendship. *Journal of Social and Personal Relationships* 1 (1984), 115–130. The types of friendship come from J. Reisman, *Anatomy of friendship* (Lexington, MA: Lewis, 1979) and J. M. Reisman, Adult friendships. In *Personal relationships. 2: Developing personal relationships,* S. Duck & R. Gilmour (eds.). New York: Academic Press, 1981 pp. 205–230. An excellent review of research and theory on friendship is W. K. Rawlins, *Friendship matters: Communication, dialectics, and the life course*. Hawthorne, NY: Aldine DeGruyter, 1992).

26. Grief-Stricken Communication

This is a topic that is discussed at length in the various grief websites. Simply search for *grief* or similar terms. The five stages of grief come from the many works of Elisabeth Kubler-Ross, for example, *On Death and Dying, Living with Death,* and *On Life after Death.* There are also numerous websites devoted to Kubler-Ross's thinking.

27. Heterosexist Talk

Heterosexist talk and homophobia generally are covered in R. J. Ringer, (Ed.), *Queer words, queer images: Communication and the construction of homosexuality* (New York: New York University Press, 1994) and J. Chesebro, (Ed.),*Gayspeak: Gay male and lesbian communication* (New York: Pilgrim Press, 1981).

28. Immediacy

The findings reported on immediacy are largely the result of research by Virginia Richmond, James McCroskey, and their colleagues and are well summarized in V. Richmond, J. C. McCroskey, & M. Hickson, *Nonverbal behavior in interpersonal relations,* 7th ed. (Boston, MA: Allyn & Bacon, 2012).

29. Introductions

The process of introducing people is covered in just about every book on etiquette. Books by "Miss Manners" are especially interesting and relevant.

30. Listening

This listening model is presented in most of my books, for example, *The Interpersonal Communication Book*

(Boston, MA: Pearson, 2013) and *Essentials of Human Communication* (Boston, MA: Pearson, 2014). The model relies on the works of a variety of researchers in listening; see, for example, J. Brownell, *Listening: Attitudes, principles, and skills,* 3d ed. (Boston: Allyn & Bacon, 2006) and D. L. Worthington, & M. E. Fitch-Hauser, *Listening: Processes, functions, and competency* (Boston: Allyn & Bacon, 2012). The fallacies of reasoning can be found in most books on argumentation and persuasion. Those I found particularly useful include: A. Pratkanis, & E. Aronson, *Age of propaganda: The everyday use and abuse of persuasion* (New York: W. H. Freeman, 1991); J. A. Herrick, *Argumentation: Understanding and shaping arguments* (State College, PA: Strata Publishing, 2004); and A. M. Lee, & E. B. Lee, *The fine art of propaganda.* (San Francisco, CA: International Society for General Semantics, 1972).

31. Listening Actively

Active listening owes most to Thomas Gordon, *P.E.T.: Parent effectiveness training.* (New York: New American Library, 1975). Gordon has written a number of other popular books using similar approaches. All are worthwhile. Also see C. Rogers, & R. Farson, (1981), Active listening. In J. A. DeVito (Ed.), *Communication: Concepts and processes* (3rd ed., pp. 137–147). (Englewood Cliffs, NJ: Prentice-Hall, 1981)

32. **Lying Detection**

The best sources on lying and lie detection are Ekman, P. (1985). *Telling lies: Clues to deceit in the marketplace, politics, and marriage.* New York: Norton and Knapp, M. L. (2008) and *Lying and deception in human interaction.* Boston: Pearson. These works detail the vast and varied research on lying and lie detection and are the major sources on which I drew for this discussion. The ways in which people lie is largely from Ekman, though various writers present somewhat similar typologies.

33. Metacommunicating

Despite its importance, little has been written on metacommunication and even less research has been conducted on its value. A somewhat more extensive treatment appears in my *The Interpersonal communication book* (Boston, MA: Pearson, 2013).

34. Mindfulness

Much has been written on mindfulness and you can find material similar to that presented here on lots of websites. But, for a good grounding in this important concept, start with E. J. Langer, *Mindfulness* (Reading, MA: Addison-Wesley, 1989).

35. Perceptual Accuracy

For research and theory on uncertainty reduction see C. R. Berger, & J. J. Bradac, *Language and social knowledge: Uncertainty in interpersonal relations* (London: Edward Arnold, 1982); D. E. Brashers, A theory of communication and uncertainty management. In *Explaining communication: Contemporary theories and exemplars* (pp. 201-218), B. B. Whaley & W. Samter (Eds.) (Mahwah, NJ: Lawrence Erlbaum, 2007); and W. Gudykunst, Toward a theory of effective interpersonal and intergroup communication: An anxiety/uncertainty management (AUM) perspective. In Wiseman, R. L., ed. *Intercultural communication competence*. Thousand Oaks, CA: Sage, 1993).

36. Politeness in Conversation

37. Politeness Online

The concept of positive and negative face owes its formulation to Erving Goffman's *Interaction ritual: Essays on face-to-face behavior* (New York, NY: Pantheon, 1967) and to P. Brown & S. C. Levinson's. *Politeness: Some universals of language usage.* Cambridge, England: Cambridge University Press, 1987). Also see J. Holmes, (1995). *Women, men and politeness* (New York, NY: Longman, 1995) and D. J. Goldsmith, (2007). Brown and Levinson's politeness theory. In *Explaining communication: Contemporary theories and exemplars* (pp. 219-236), B. B. Whaley, & W. Samter (Eds.). (Mahwah, NJ: Lawrence Erlbaum, 2007). The six maxims of politeness are from Geoffrey Leech (1983). *Principles of pragmatics.* London: Longman. An excellent guide to politeness in everyday communication is offered by P. M. Forni, *Choosing Civility: The twentyfive rules of considerate conduct.* NY: St. Martin's Griffin, 2002. For the cultural maxims see K. Midooka, Characteristics of Japanese style communication. Media, Culture and Society, 12 (October, 1990), 477–489 and Y. Gu, Polite phenomena in modern Chinese. *Journal of Pragmatics,* 14 (1997), 237–257.

38. Power

The six types of power owe their formulation to J. R. P. French, Jr., & B. Raven, (1968). The bases of social power. In *Group dynamics: Research and theory,* 3d ed., D. Cartwright & A. Zander (eds.) (New York: Harper & Row, 1968), pp. 259–269 and B. Raven, B., C. Centers, & A. Rodrigues, (1975). The bases of conjugal power. In *Power in families,* R. E. Cromwell & D. H. Olson (eds.) (New York: Halsted Press, 1975), pp. 217–234. Also see B. H. Raven, J. Schwarzwald, & M. Koslowsky, M. Conceptualizing and measuring a power/interaction model of interpersonal influence. *Journal of Applied Social Psychology* 28 (1998),

307–332. Research on the downside of coercive power is presented in V. P. Richmond, & J. C. McCroskey, Power in the classroom II: Power and learning. *Communication Education* 33 (1984), 125–136.

39. Relationship Development
40. Relationship Deterioration
41. Relationship Dissolution
42. Relationship Repair

Among the most comprehensive sources are M. L. Knapp, & A. Vangelisti, *Interpersonal communication and human relationships,* 6th ed. (Boston, MA: Allyn & Bacon, 2009); L. K. Guerrero, P. A., Andersen, P. A., & W. A. Afifi, *Close encounters: Communication in relationships,* 2nd ed. (Thousand Oaks, CA: Sage, 2007); S. Duck, *Human relationships* (Thousand Oaks, CA: Sage, 1986). On relationship repair see B. L. Duncan, & J. W. Rock, *Overcoming relationship impasses: Ways to initiate change when your partner won't help* (New York: Plenum Press/ Insight Books, 1991). The notion of cherishing behaviors is from W. J. Lederer, *Creating a good relationship* (New York: Norton, 1984) and W. J. Lederer, & D. D. Jackson, *The mirages of marriage* (New York: Norton, 1968).

43. Self-Awareness

For the Johari window see J. Luft, *Of human interaction* (3rd ed.) (Palo Alto, CA: Mayfield, 1969) and J. Luft, *Group process: An introduction of group dynamics* (3rd ed.). Palo Alto, CA: Mayfield, 1984).

44. Self-Disclosing
45. Self-Disclosing: Facilitation and Responding
46. Self-disclosing: Resisting

The research on self-disclosure in communication and psychology is extensive. Much of the research began with Sidney Jourard's work; see his *Disclosing man to himself (*New York: Van Nostrand Reinhold, 1968) and *Self-disclosure* (Hoboken, NJ: Wiley, 1971). For the value of self-disclosure in mental and physical health see J. W. Pennebacker, *Opening up: The healing power of confiding in others* (New York: Morrow, 1991). For a summary of gender differences see V. S. Helgeson, *Psychology of gender,* 3rd ed. (Upper Saddle River, NJ: Prentice-Hall, 2009). Also see S. Sprecher, & S. S. Hendrick, Self-disclosure in intimate relationships: Associations with individual and relationship characteristics over time. *Journal of Social and Clinical Psychology* 23 (December, 2004), 857-877.

47. Self-Esteem

The self-destructive beliefs are from P. E. Butler, *Talking to yourself: Learning the language of self-support*. New York: Harper & Row, 1981). Also see C. Rogers, (1970). *Carl Rogers on encounter groups* (New York: Harrow Books, 1970) and J. Van Praagh, (2010). I am! I can! I will! (www.healyourlife.com).

48. Small Talk

There's a great deal written on small talk but virtually no research. A useful little book is M. Wadsworth (2005). *Small talk savvy.* Avon, MA: Adams Media.

49. Violence Management

The best sources I've found on violence are college and university websites that offer advice to students on dealing with violence. These sites aren't selling anything and are often the most reliable. One excellent one is www.utexas.edu/student/cmhc/booklets/relavio/relaviol.html.

50. Workplace Communication

The best sources for suggestions on workplace communication are the various websites that identify specific workplace skills, e.g., interviewing, mentoring, and networking. My *The Interviewing Guidebook*, 2nd ed. (Boston, MA: Pearson, 2010) covers many of these strategies.